For a while, James Ball supposed the ringing was a part of his dreaming – a delegation of bell-ringers of the traditional Sussex kind on the tarmac of Melbourne Airport, perhaps – and only slowly did the ringing become divorced from the dreaming. Eventually it became impossible to dream away the fact of a strident bedside telephone.

'Is that you, James?' The voice of Sir Hector Bootle blasted away the last kindly cobwebs of slumber. 'I hope you're in a fit state to get down here at the double. Something really frightful has turned up, or rather gone missing. You can charge us for a taxi.'

'Where are you, Hector?'

'At Lord's, of course,' the Senior Security Adviser thundered. Then he added in an abrupt whisper, 'In the Museum, in fact.'

'It's not a very nice night,' James gently protested.

'It's a disastrous night for England!' Sir Hector snapped. 'I will expect you here in five minutes.' Then the telephone went dead.

Also in Arrow by Allen Synge

BOWLER, BATSMAN, SPY

with Leo Cooper

TALES FROM FAR PAVILIONS
BEYOND THE FAR PAVILIONS

HUNTERS
of the
LOST ASHES

Allen Synge

ARROW BOOKS

Arrow Books Limited
62–65 Chandos Place, London WC2N 4NW

An imprint of Century Hutchinson Limited

London Melbourne Sydney Auckland
Johannesburg and agencies throughout
the world

First published by George Weidenfeld & Nicolson Ltd 1987

Arrow edition 1988
© Allen Synge 1987

Phototypeset by Input Typesetting Ltd, London

Printed and bound in Great Britain by
Anchor Brendon Limited, Tiptree, Essex

ISBN 0 09 955980 3

For Frances and Bernard
in their wedding year

'Life is a conspiracy to prevent one
from watching cricket.'

The Author

HUNTERS
of the
LOST ASHES

Prologue

Melbourne, 1932

Dad always said cricket was the noblest of sports. Always told me a man could win no greater honour on life's weary way than to represent his State against the flower of England; apart, that was, from the opportunity to represent Australia against the same chivalrous enemy.

He was beside me that day at the MCG before I walked to the middle in my first match for the State against England. Just the crease in their flannel trousers was enough to make you feel humbled by the honour that had been bestowed on you. 'Play a straight bat, son,' Dad called from the Family and Friends Stand. 'Show 'em we're not provincials here in Melbourne. Show 'em we've got the classy strokes too!'

Take 'two legs' and notice Umpire George Hele is smiling. Notice it because he's the only man on the field who *is* smiling. Notice another thing too: the field is switching round. 'Give the cherry to Lol, Gubby!' Their skipper calls to the pom with the centre parting who's just beginning his run up. 'More his meat than yours, I think.'

Try to take in their placings, but they're all moving about. A whole army of blue caps crowding the leg side – their skipper so close you can smell the Wrights Cold Tar Soap on his alabaster cheeks.

Umpire Hele is still smiling; but the bloke behind him isn't. He's running in silent as nightfall and his eyes are saying he wants to kill me, even though we've never met.

And suddenly the ball is here, rising fast towards my scalp – just as I'm shaping for an off-drive like Mr Hammond's, just as Dad told me. I start to move my right leg to the off, try to get my bat off the perpendicular for the hook. But now it's too late for hooking, too late for ducking. Oh Jesus, I never realised cricket could hurt so much!

Come to in another place. I say it feels like hell, but my mates say it's the Victorian dressing room. And in the doorway there's this angel of death. English. Captain. Can't somehow put a name to him. Mr Woodfull is saying he's not wanted here, but he won't go away. Lips mouthing polite English words of commiseration. Eyes saying you got your just desserts, you despicable little colonial!

The cobbers are asking how are you feeling, are you all right there old son? And I start to nod my head and say, 'I'm fine, just dinkum.' But I know and they know it'll never be the same, not for me, not for them, not for anyone in the whole putrid world.

Splinters in a Museum

1

It was no night for cricket in St John's Wood. The wind was howling like a Millwall invasion and the force of it was strong enough to throw dead leaves and the scarlet shreds of dahlias against the windows with the violence of a Chelsea supporter.

'Oh not to be in England now that *Match of the Day* is here!' James Ball had joked wryly over the *Radio Times* some days ago. And this was before the autumn rains came and England lost 3-nil to Northern Ireland in an endlessly replayed fiasco at Wembley!

There is light at the end of the darkest tunnel, and in the Balls' case it was happily not too far away. A few feet from the marriage bed gleamed the plasticised leather and copper-plate locks of a new suitcase, already half filled with lingerie, bikinis, and diaphanous summer wear bought by Jan Ball at generous discounts from Harrods and Harvey Nichols. And on the bedside table of the retired spymaster a colourful brochure had just been set down, packed with marsupials, bronzed surf riders, nubile Sheilas, and unusually welcoming-looking aborigines and sunsets or dawns bringing flushes to a famous bridge and a notable opera house.

In other words, the Balls were shortly leaving for

Australia to realise a long-cherished dream for James and make possible an overdue change of air for Jan.

An advertisement in the *Cricketer* had first amused them, then tempted them and finally proved irresistible. It was the headline that had produced the initial smiles: FOLLOW ENGLAND'S ASHES QUEST WITH WALLY FICKET!

'Should we know Mr Wally Ficket?' James had queried laconically.

'Darling, your memory must be going,' Jan had gently teased. 'Can you ever forget the Third Test at Headingley against Australia?'

'Ah yes, the batsman/wicketkeeper who didn't exactly shine in either department.'

'He was hopeless in *every* department,' Jan had added with an earthy laugh which she had abruptly cut short. Too many tears for domestic comfort had been spilled over her weakness for men in white flannels.

'Jan is feeling much more at home with the flat and me,' James had been telling his friends for over a year now.

A momentary embarrassment was resolved by mutual appreciation of the advertisement copy. This is what it had promised.

With ex-England and Derbyshire star, Wally Ficket, as your guide, escape from the English winter on a once-in-a-lifetime tour of Australia following Gatting's MCC Cricketers. You and your partner will have a ringside seat at all the famous Test grounds where the battle for the historic Ashes is to be joined. Plus complimentary passes to the major One-Day Internationals. At all six Tests you will have the benefit of Wally's expert insights into the game at the highest level, and at informal social occasions you will have the opportunity to discuss the 'state of play' with personalities drawn from Wally's wide range of contacts in both dressing rooms. Thrill to Tests with Wally Ficket! But also thrill to the experience of Australia! Its fabulous beaches . . . Its legendary outback . . . Its vibrant lifestyle and infectiously friendly people. . . .

There was more of this, but Jan's eyes had now sliced through the rhetoric to the price: 'Kangaroo Tours offers you all this for only £999.95 (inc. luxury hotel accommodation and grandstand seats)!'

'Why, that's less than we'd spend on central heating if this winter is anything like it promises to be!' she exclaimed.

'We pay on the Easy Gas Plan,' James had reminded her.

'I'm sure Kangaroo Tours have an easy plan, too.'

'I don't want to seem ungallant, but the harsh fact is we are OAPs, my love – index-linked, admittedly, but you can never tell with this Chancellor.' And then James had added dreamily, 'I've never seen Melbourne, I mean the cricket ground. I think it must be quite a revelation.'

' "Come fly with me!" ' Jan had hummed smilingly, an allusion to Sinatra's mid-50s *Songs for Swinging Lovers*, and a brief but glowing period of re-kindled ardour in the relationship. And that had settled it.

A telephone call to Kangaroo Tours. The forms and brochures by return of post. Within forty-eight hours the whole thing had been arranged.

So now, while the wind outside howled like Prime Minister's Question Time, the couple were resting on the threshold of Australia. Hand in hand, if not cheek to cheek, they were nodding into a sleep that was nosing ahead of the QANTAS Boeing: a dreamy carrier

15

wafting them backwards in the direction of Lindwall and Miller, Bradman and Ponsford, Trumper and Spofforth – back into summer and green fields and white flannels, back, in a sense, in time. For when people become a little older, they tend to count their aging in winters, tend to trace their comparative decay by the football seasons Father Time remorselessly beckons them towards.

Yet now the Balls were facing the stern old bail-collector with an emphatic rejection. Even though they were half asleep, they were already slipping away from him, escaping with Wally Ficket into the vibrant, youthful summer of Australia, leaving Father Time to spin on his axis above the scoreboard at Lord's in a wind screaming like a demonstration of 'Women for Peace'.

For a while, James Ball supposed the ringing was a part of his dreaming – a delegation of bell-ringers of the traditional Sussex kind on the tarmac of Melbourne Airport, perhaps – and only slowly did the ringing become divorced from the dreaming. Eventually it became impossible to dream away the fact of a strident bedside telephone.

'Is that you, James?'

'No, he's gone to Australia.'

'Have you been drinking or something, James?'

'Only at the fountain of comparative youth.'

The voice of Sir Hector Bootle blasted away the last kindly cobwebs of slumber.

'I hope you're in a fit state to get down here at the double. Something really frightful has turned up, or rather gone missing. You can charge us for a taxi, I suppose, but from where you are you might as well walk.'

16

'Where are you Hector?'

'At Lord's, of course,' the Senior Security Adviser thundered. Then he added in an abrupt whisper, 'In the museum, in fact.'

'It's not a very nice night,' James gently protested.

'It's a disastrous night for England!' Sir Hector snapped. 'I will expect you here in five minutes.' Then the telephone went dead.

2

> The body will be cremated, and the
> Ashes taken to Australia.

So concluded the satirical obituary for English cricket published in the *Sporting Times* of the week ending 1 September 1882 which, as far as records go, is where the legend of the 'Ashes' begins. In strictest orthodoxy, the Ashes are a mythical concept; but some people are convinced they have tangible form. A small rosewood urn is enshrined under glass in the Museum at Lord's, and those people who venerate it and who also happen to be Australians can never fully understand why this sacred relic is not transferred to Sydney or Melbourne, or tactfully rotated between the two, whenever the Ashes are wrested from England.

The answer, of course, is that the Urn is a deeply symbolic gift to England from Australia presented by a Miss Florrie Morphy of Sunbury, Victoria, to the triumphant English captain of the 1882–83 tour, the Hon. Ivo Bligh who was shortly to make her his wife and his Lady when he inherited the title of eighth Earl of Darnley.

17

The Urn is thought to contain the ashes of an Australian cricket stump, bail or conceivably ball, barbecued or sacrificed by the bewitching Miss Morphy in honour of her future Master and Lord. There are other theories as to the nature of the ashes the Urn contains, but these need not trouble us just now. The fact of the matter is that ever since the Lord's Cricket Museum was established in the late 1950s, Lady Darnley's Ashes Urn, previously housed in the Long Room, has been its centrepiece.

And there can be no doubt that a kind of magic, a certain whiff of mystery and sanctity emanates from the glass showcase in which the Urn and its velvet pouch are reverently preserved. There is an old saying, dating perhaps from a period when St John's Wood still had elms and oaks and a rural tradition, which clearly warns:

> Spill the butter, break the churn;
> But Lord help harvest if we lose the Urn!

It was this old superstitious fear, or a modern echo of it, that purple-faced Sir Hector Bootle was now violently voicing to James.

It had been disturbing to find policemen checking credentials at the Grace Gate, ringing the Pavilion and, in particular, crowding the entrance to the Museum. James Ball had never seen so many policemen at Lord's, not even at a Nat West Cup Final. An additional force of Metropolitan officers, or draftees from the Counties, were ranged on the staircase to the Museum's main exhibits, as if this howling night was some kind of Royal Command Performance. One half expected to glimpse tiaras instead of

18

the normal displays of weathered bats and the celebrity-less caps and regalia of the Test playing nations.

But there were celebrities here of a kind. Among them for instance, though his back was turned and his head and shoulders were sunk in dumb despair, James could recognise the slim silhouette of J. Spriggs, Secretary of the MCC. Behind him paced the grey and lanky shape of Sir Wilfred Breslau, the Club's Senior Antiquarian. Not usually a smoking man, he was moving now in a kind of vapour and in his footsteps were little grey piles of a substance that would soon make international headlines. For the glass case containing the authentic Ashes was smashed. The Urn and its velvet pouch were gone. The floor sparkled with glass splinters.

The horror and impiety of the act seemed to have communicated itself not only to the distinguished men who stood or paced broken around the shattered case, but also the Museum's inanimate objects. There was a look of furtive terror in the eyes of the giant photographic blow-ups of Grace, Bradman and J. B. Hobbs, as if they were trying to say, We've seen something all right, but we daren't tell!

Sir Hector Bootle, the Prime Minister's Senior Security Adviser, was not one of the exhibits. This was clear from his florid and quivery features and the resonant words which were issuing from him.

'What I want to know, James, is are we contemplating a break-in or an inside job?'

'The Museum was presumably locked?'

'The lock was smashed by a bullet from a Walther P38; but that proves nothing, as you really ought to know, James. In fact, as you should be telling me, the more dramatic the entry the more justified one is in

19

suspecting an inside job.' Sir Hector shot a molten glance at the bowed MCC officials.

'I was dining at my club,' protested the Secretary. 'Not this Club, of course – the Bath.' He added in a bruised undertone, 'I can produce witnesses but I would scarcely think that would be necessary.'

'Is there a janitor or a cleaning lady who keeps a key?' James enquired routinely.

'That's another fishy thing about this whole damned business,' Sir Hector boomed. 'It seems there's an old harpy called Mrs Sandham who's responsible for mopping up here. It now transpires she's gone missing. Her daughter says she's playing bingo in Hammersmith, but I'm taking that with a very large pinch of salt. In fact, the moment we can lay hands on her, I'm packing the old bundle into "the cage" at Harpenden. She'll sing like a linnet after a weekend in!'

' "The cage" at Harpenden? Hector, I appreciate this is serious, but you're surely not treating it as a matter of National Security?'

'Don't be so wet, James,' the Senior Security official reprimanded. 'In fact you *are* wet. Look, you're making puddles all over the floor.'

'It's raining outside, Hector,' Ball patiently reminded him, 'and if you remember, you counselled against a cab. As it happened, there wasn't one.'

'What I meant, James, was what a bloody wet question. Is this a matter of National Security? Of course it damned well is! I should have thought even you would be able to see the disastrous repercussions this thing is going to have on England's tour of Australia. You were a Cambridge Blue, weren't you? You shouldn't need me to tell you that cricketers are an extraordinarily superstitious bunch. After their drubbing by Western Australia this thing is going to hit Gatting's chaps like a kick in the face.'

'But a matter of National Security?' James gamely persisted.

'Of course, if you want to be pedantic about it, the answer is that strictly speaking I'm acting *ex-officio*, as a Member of the MCC at the request of my Committee.' Sir Hector fired a glance at the bereft Club Secretary who gave a numb nod of confirmation. 'Yes, if you insist on reading the small print of my terms of reference, I can confirm that the Prime Minister is not involved in this enquiry. I am acting as an expert consultant, unpaid, in the interests of my club and my country, which is the basis on which I'm expecting you to work, James.'

What an unpredictable honour a knighthood is, James reflected. For some civil servants it can be an ennobling catalyst, turning a mundane busy-body into a relaxed, charming and sometimes, even, cultured individual. With others it can have the effect of magnifying the least appealing traits, accentuating coarseness and eliminating any sensitivity the unknighted personality may have owned. Hector Bootle's knighthood had placed him, it had sadly to be admitted, in the second category. But then it had never been clearly established where he had been at school. These were the thoughts which passed through James's mind as he braced himself to face the tense Security official with the facts of his situation.

'The payment is not so much a concern as the problem of my availability,' he finally answered. 'You see, I'm taking Jan to Australia the day after tomorrow.' He checked his wristwatch. 'Or, rather, tomorrow as it is now. We're going to see the Tests

21

together. Jan has been looking forward to the trip like a child, Hector. I couldn't disappoint her now.'

'I'm sorry, James, but I can't have you running off to Australia at a time like this. I'm looking to you to summon up your last ounce of professional nous and tell me who's got their nasty thieving hands on the Ashes. Besides, I can't see that it makes any sense at all to risk Jan in Australia. You know perfectly well what happens to her when she so much as sniffs a green cap.'

'Did I hear someone mention Australia?' The interruption came from the direction of a mountain-ringed representation of the cricket ground at Tobago, and from behind an advancing screen of cigarette smoke the crumpled shape of Sir Wilfred Breslau, the Club's Senior Antiquarian, re-materialised. 'Now you mention Australia,' he coughed, 'I'm reminded of the last occasion we lost the Ashes – was it under Denness in '73–'74, or Willis in '82–'83? – no matter. The point is, I clearly remember some very unsavoury individuals wearing those cowboy hats they have in Queensland hanging around the Museum with every intent of creating mischief. In fact, now I recollect, they were doing more than looking threatening. I could not understand what they were shouting myself, but my secretary, who had spent a little time in Australia, translated for me. 'Return the Ashes to Greg and the boys or we will come and collect them ourselves!' was, I understand, the tenor of their demands. I took the precaution of ringing the Head Groundsman for as many burly lads with picks and shovels as he could spare, and that clearly helped to diffuse the situation. But the point I'm making is: cannot we discern in this earlier incident a clue to the culprits responsible for tonight's act of vandalism? Indeed, gentlemen, is it not reasonable to surmise that the author or authors of this atrocity have Australasian origins?'

'Mr Border has certainly given it out that he expects to regain the Ashes this time,' the Club and Ground Administrator, Admiral Chester Fishlock, reflected. 'I think it's quite possible that certain hotheads among the Earl's Court fraternity, inflamed by Western Australia's convincing win over our Touring Party – and incidentally, let's not read too much into this, our men need time to find their land legs – and, no doubt, by liberal indulgence in the native brew, have decided to take the law into their own hands and perpetrate a crime which has all the hallmarks of the colonial at his most bestial.'

'Chief Inspector!' thundered Sir Hector Bootle. 'Have we gathered evidence to suggest that the man or men we are looking for are Australian?'

A silvery official came to attention under a painting of top-hatted cricketers in a bygone meadow. 'Nothing as yet, Sir Hector; but I would point out that the Walther 38 is a weapon in international use.'

'Ernie Tyburn!' the Senior Antiquarian hoarsely exclaimed.

'I beg your pardon?' rasped Sir Hector Bootle.

Sir Wilfred excitedly crammed another cigarette into his mouth. 'The Australian one-day cricket impressario. I only mention his name because it just so happens that I filed a cutting the other day that could have a vital bearing on this theft. Do I have it here? No, of course I filed it; but the gist of the report was this: in an interview with Mr Michael Parkinson it seems that Mr Tyburn expressed himself of the opinion that the Ashes Urn belongs in Australia as surely as the Elgin Marbles belong in Greece!'

'Can you believe anything that loathsome little vulgarian says?' Admiral Fishlock growled.

'Quite, quite,' impatiently continued Sir Wilfred amid a splintering of Swan Vesta matches. 'But surely the point is that this wretched man, however dispicable his character, has issued a form of licence for larceny – a dubious licence if you like, but one that has gained a kind of spurious validity through the fact that his provocative remarks have gone largely uncensored by the Australian media. Directly or indirectly, gentlemen, can we not see the hand of Tyburn in the crime we are contemplating here, tonight?'

A near silence fell on the Museum, one broken only by the continued pacing footsteps of anxious men of power. It was the Secretary of the MCC who finally spoke.

'If he can steal our cricketers, I can't see any reason why he shouldn't try and steal our Ashes. In fact, now one comes to think of it, the Urn could be just the thing Mr Tyburn needs to add a kind of bogus veneer of respectability to his disreputable show.'

'Ernie Tyburn! Why didn't you think of him before, James?' Sir Hector Bootle thigh-slapped. 'You know as well as I do that we have a file as thick as an encyclopedia on him – and one thing that file makes crystal clear is that nasty little gold-digger doesn't open his mouth to Michael Parkinson or anyone else unless he has some nefarious undertaking in mind.'

'Is there anyone we can trust to act for us in Australia?' anxiously demanded the Senior Antiquarian. 'Unless we recover the Ashes we have lost our main source of Museum revenue.'

'Mr Kerry Packer has rendered the Club considerable service recently in helping to keep Tyburn's

24

recruiting agents at bay,' revealed the Secretary, J. Spriggs, 'but to ask for his good offices in a matter which, let us admit it, is always going to be something of a sore point with our Australian friends could be putting an unfair strain on the relationship.'

'There's only one answer to this,' said Sir Hector Bootle. 'You'll have to go to Australia, James.'

'I *am* going to Australia, Hector.'

'That's right, so you are; but now you're going, at your own expense of course, with the full authority of the Club and myself. When can you leave?'

'By the first flight tomorrow,' James said, looking at the watery suggestion of morning that was beginning to light the Museum's eastern windows.

'Good. But for heaven's sake go carefully. Friend Tyburn has some extremely ugly friends. And if I were you, I'd leave Jan at home.'

James gave a noncommittal nod and moved towards the policeman-flanked staircase.

'God speed you!' Sir Wilfred Breslau called hoarsely after him. 'I'd give my right arm to see my Urn back in safe keeping!'

James descended the staircase of the stricken Museum, past grim, saluting policemen, and walked circumspectly towards the Grace Gate in order to avoid the puddles. So, he thought, it's still Australia for Jan and me. He gave a small sigh expressive of profound relief. They were still walking away from the English winter, heading backwards towards cricket and summer, still cheating Father Time. He gave another small sigh, but this was not of relief. This sigh was a whisper of conscience.

James was now unofficially as well as officially retired. Even Sir Hector Bootle had admitted as much. All the same, he wondered if ever in his life before he had failed to report a crucial piece of evidence. He asked himself if a younger James would have let officialdom rush to conclusions about the Australian connection with the theft when an alternative theory was staring them in the face?

As the men of power had paced, smoked and argued around the Urn's violated case, James had run a discreet but professional eye over the damage. His attention had first been attracted by the arrangement of the glass splinters, which fortunately had been ringed with chalk at the Chief Inspector's orders to facilitate police photography and to discourage tampering. Here was not the usual haphazard fragmentation of glass, such as might result from a small explosive mechanism or a powerfully aimed hammer or mallet. The splinters had a pattern: that of a violently but precisely divided rectangle. And this had made Ball curious about the damage sustained to the upper wooden frame of the showcase. A bomb or a hammer blow would have splintered it. A saw or a chisel would have left tell-tale evidence of its cutting edge. In fact, the frame had been sundered at the halfway mark too cleanly for any bomb or tool.

James had let his mind travel the world for a parallel example of clean force applied to solid objects. His musings had taken him all the way to the Far East before he was certain he had a satisfactory explanation. The damage sustained to the Ashes showcase was entirely and *only* consistent with a karate chop.

Underground to Down Under

Barons Court, Hammersmith, Acton Town . . . what
had they to do with the great Test arenas of Brisbane,
Sydney and Mebourne? The answer, of course, was
that they were stations on the Piccadilly Line to
Heathrow. The new 'tube to plane' link had soldered
these unfashionable suburbs onto the total experience
of Australia – or India or Venezuela, for that matter.
It was odd, James thought, how the way to the world
had come to lie through South Ealing.

Jan had said they really ought to take a taxi because
of the luggage, and it was true they had now accumu-
lated four separate pieces – three large suitcases
packed with Jan's things, one for James's effects. But
James had felt bound to point out that a cab all the
way to Heathrow, taking into account the scale of tips
that would be involved, would eat up almost a week's
pension, albeit index-linked. Jan had said what the
hell? – or words to that effect – it was a once-in-a-
lifetime excursion. So finally a compromise had been
reached: a taxi to Leicester Square for the tube
connection followed, as it had turned out, by an
exhausting plunge down the escalator, which was out
of order, and a difficult boarding operation into a late
rush-hour train.

Now with the main stations of commerce passed,
the passengers were beginning to thin out and it was
possible to stack some of the luggage on vacated seats.

James even felt relaxed enough to open the morning papers.

'You really ought to save them for the plane,' Jan said.

'I've got the new Le Carré for that. Besides . . .' It hardly needed stressing that the theft of the Ashes Urn from the Lord's Museum had made all the front pages, notwithstanding the fact that Sir Hector Bootle had given strict instructions that the incident was on no account to be leaked to the media.

'ASHES BREAK IN WHO BLUNDERED?' the *Daily Mail* wanted to know.

The *Daily Mirror* led with a moving personal appeal from Sir Robert Maxwell for the return of the Urn either to the MCC or the *Mirror* offices.

The *Guardian* contained a lightish piece by Frank Keating, a profound thought-piece by its regular cricket correspondent, Matthew Engel, and a richly evocative piece from John Arlott in his Channel Islands retirement quoting a little-known traditional Middlesex couplet.

> Let cow get foot-mould, let hayrick burn,
> But Heaven help t'arvest if we lose the Urn!

The leader suggested that the loss of the Ashes could, in a deeply symbolic way, prove a more severe blow to the Conservative Government's credibility than the latest unemployment figures. 'We remain a perversely superstitious people; we have, perhaps, an inordinate reverence for our superiors and betters. But we expect them to be efficient custodians of our national shrines.'

The Times, in a thoughtful front page article (continued on page 13), discreetly explored the possibility of an Australian connection and went so far as to remind readers of Mr Ernie Tyburn's assertion that Australia's claim to the Ashes Urn was at least as convincing as that of Athens to the Elgin Marbles. The article was responsible for renewed pinpricks of irritation on the skin of James's conscience. While he was perfectly willing to admit the possibility of an Australian connection, he knew in his heart that it had been unprofessional to leave England without drawing the attention of some rational person in authority to the evidence of the karate chop. It was to cover this secret embarrassment that he turned to the obituaries.

It came as a shock, and since a shock can sometimes be a form of relief, a dubious kind of diversion to note that young L. M. S. Partridge had died. The obituary dwelt on his contribution to the Oxford XIs of the late '50s and the never-quite-wholly-fulfilled promise he had shown for England, as exemplified by a spirited knock of 48 in the rain-affected Lord's Test of 1964 and a memorable top-spinner that had dislodged Bobby Simpson's off bail. The obituary passed briefly over Partridge's short but sensational tenure as Chairman of the England selectors ('a less than happy period in a life marked by much achievement') and regretted, without being specific, the circumstances of his last days. 'Alas, the innings was not completed in a manner which his old friends had been entitled to expect,' it concluded, leaving the question open whether this sorry victim of KGB intrigue of a few Test series back had died of drink, disreputable women or suicide.

The other featured demise was also a distantly familiar name to James – Sir Gervase Spooner whose death a fortnight earlier on the Coburn Peninsula of the Arafura Sea had just come to the attention of the column. The life of Spooner, whom Ball had met once or twice in the war and perhaps once in the immediate post-war period, had odd parallels with that of L. M. S. Partridge. A career of promising beginnings as a young scientist involved in secret and unspecified war work had been recognised in an unusual way by promotion to Chief of Security at Buckingham Palace. *The Times* explained Sir Gervase's early retirement, shortly after the Coronation, to Australia's remote northern coastline as 'the call of a life-long interest in Far Eastern studies'. However, as with the luckless L. M. S. Partridge, the obituarist had serious if oblique reservations about Sir Gervase's final phase: 'The world began to beat a path to his door and older friends who had known him in his Swindon days, might have wished he had chosen an even remoter fastness.'

Northfields, Boston Manor, Osterley . . . Australia was getting closer with every Piccadilly Line station, the moment of take off only a matter of stops away. As distraction from the uneasiness in the heart or the soul, wherever it is located, came the faint rustle of butterflies in the stomach. Not the genuine palpitating feeling of waiting on a wartime airstrip, parachute harness on the back, nor the similar sensation of some years earlier of waiting on a Victoria Station platform with bucket and spade for the train to the sea and Brighton and Hove and Maurice Tate and A. E. R. Gilligan. These stomach flutters were only a hushed echo of the former feelings. All the same, James Ball was glad to discover he was excited by the prospect of the flight.

'Darling, why is that Chinese gentleman taking pictures of you?' Jan was asking.

James looked along the carriage. A smiling oriental tourist appeared to be snapping a kimono-clad wife and daughter.

'Actually he is a Japanese gentleman, my love, and he seems to be photographing his family.'

'And you when you're not looking,' Jan hissed.

'I can't see why he would want to do that.'

'Exactly. You're not the most photogenic face in London, are you my sweet?' Jan said in an undertone.

'I think you're imagining things.'

'I think you should pretend to be reading your paper – and wait and see.'

James turned to John Woodcock's assessment of the MCC's prospects against South Australia. *The Times* doyen was reasonably confident that Gatting's men would find an easier wicket at Adelaide than they had encountered at Perth and would be facing a less demanding attack. If Gatting was to prove lucky with the toss and (always assuming he took the decision to bat) Broad and Athey were to give the MCC innings a solid start, Woodcock was hopeful that the England party would be able to build the first respectable total of the tour, providing, he stressed, that there were no more defections to Ernie Tyburn's one-day caravan.

A Canon camera flashed, and out of the corner of his eye James saw that the now unsmiling Japanese tourist had him and no one else in his sights. And his was not the most photogenic face in London, as Jan had pointed out.

Adelaide Overture

Sebastian Gover was sitting high up in the press box above Adelaide's November-green Oval. Today he was no longer a shadowy figure behind the famous media faces. For the first time in his life he was rubbing shoulders with Blofeld and Robin Marlar. No more craning for a view behind the backs of the household names. From where Sebastian Gover was sitting, it was possible to press his nose against the box's glass pane or exhale onto its surface the shimmering imprint of his breath, for he was occupying the seat usually reserved for the *Observer*'s senior cricket correspondent.

It was Sebastian Gover's fortune that Scyld Berry of the *Observer* had been confined to his hotel bedroom by his paper to write a whole page feature on the Lord's Ashes theft. As an occasional contributor to the distinguished Sunday's club cricket columns, Gover had been chosen to report on the South Australia game, since he happened to be in Australia on behalf of a number of south-east England local papers.

One thing was already noticeable about the new man from the *Observer*: his typewriter was working faster than Blofeld's or Roebuck's, Engel's or Marks' (the other Somerset player turned wordsmith). 'Scyld had better look to his laurels,' Tony Lewis confided to the *Daily Telegraph*'s Michael Carey in a smiling whisper. But the truth was that young Sebastian

Gover had even bigger game in his sights. Neville Cardus and Alan Ross had always been his inspiration and his idols, but they would shortly have to make room in their pantheon to accommodate an even more significant talent.

'Under the blue streak of the Mount Lofty range, Small bounds into bowl,' his typewriter pounded:

A whirling black and white blur, aiming to knock South Australia's batting order black and blue. Hilditch goes forward on the front foot, solid as an Australian burgundy but lacking perhaps the bouquet of the real thing. Meanwhile Dilley from the pavilion end finds lift with deliveries which impressively reverse the grim laws of gravity. Haysman, baton waving as imperiously as Solti, conducts a brief scherzo outside his off stump. Rhodes's appeal is loud enough to disturb the swans on the Torrens river. But Umpire Timmins remains as impassive as a Picasso still life.

Sebastian Gover was taking his opportunity with both hands. All the same, as the day wore on, it became obvious that the cricket was falling well below the intense quality of the writing. The truth of the matter was that the Adelaide Oval was practically deserted. ('Stands like open mouths,' Sebastian had written in a deleted paragraph, 'wait for the dentist's filling.') At the same time it could not be said that the ground was hushed. In fact, it would have been technically impossible for Rhodes's appeal to have disturbed a single swan on the Torrens river, because they had been routed by the super-amplified clamour of voice and brass that was emanating from a brand new stadium beyond the cathedral. As every citizen of Adelaide could not fail to be aware, Ernie Tyburn's Australian All Stars XI was engaged in a one-day 'Megatest' against a team of South African rebels.

There was no question as to which event was proving the bigger draw. As Australia's renegade Test hero, Greg Mountain, danced down the wicket in his green Spiderman outfit to power-drive a six into the Day-glo pavilion, fifty-five thousand throats roared; then randily cheered as scantily-clad Ernie Tyburn hostesses cart-wheeled onto the wicket to plant succulent kisses on the striker's rugged cheek.

And this was only one of the refinements the Australian multi-millionaire and impressario had introduced to the game once called cricket. At Ernie Tyburn fixtures, spectators had the opportunity to follow two quite different types of illuminated scoreboard. One showed the runs scored and overs bowled, the other recorded the batsmen's earnings, stroke by stroke. This six by Greg Mountain, for instance, had just pushed his total takings for the season up to the $Aus200,000 mark, winning him, as the board flashily signalled, a 'jackpot' payout of a further $Aus5,000 and another round of smacking kisses from Tyburn's leggy glamour line-up. Of course, there were forfeits as well as prizes: a dropped catch sent a player's personal earnings score spinning into reverse to the tune of $Aus1,000 and brought down on his head the risible award of The Golden Pudding Basin from now contemptuous Tyburn scantily-clads. A single-figure score merited another cash deduction and the award of a monster pair of bifocals by the delectable referees. A 'duck' saw the wretched batsman pursued around the field by a posse of Disneyland figures. Bowlers were eligible for other incentives and penalties, as the South African rebel pace man, Garth Smuts, was now demonstrating. He had just managed to send down a maiden over to Greg Mountain's partner, Wayne Rockface. Now, fittingly, he was accorded the favour of a brief symbolic tumble with a Tyburn hostess. The crowd applauded even louder than they had for Greg Mountain's six.

'Gatting tosses the ball to Edmonds and a ripple of expectancy runs round the crowd, like the Torrence river at spring tide,' typed Sebastian Gover back in the orthodoxy of the Adelaide Oval press box; but he knew in his heart he was building sentences without straw. Silently he damned his idols Neville Cardus and Alan Ross. At no moment in their careers, let alone on the day when fate had handed them their big chance, had either had to compete with an Ernie Tyburn one-day Megatest.

The Voyage Out

1

A heavily built man in an England sweater moved, pewter tankard in hand, to the centre of the departure lounge.

'No need to panic, ladies and gents,' he announced. 'The skipper informs us it was just a bit of dodgy luggage the security mob were not too happy about. They've got it out of the plane now and are giving it the old once-over for explosive material. Let's hope it's not that new bikini you were saving for Bondi beach, eh Granny?' He winked in Jan Ball's direction. 'Seriously though, they'll be loading the regular passengers in about half an hour and our party shortly afterwards. In an hour we should all be airborne and outward bound for the land of the amber liquid. But let me introduce myself. My name is Wally Ficket, formerly of Derbyshire and England for my sins, and now your honoured guide, philosopher and fellow convivialist on the Test tour to end them all!

'We're going to have plenty of occasions to get acquainted,' the ex-wicketkeeper/batsman promised. 'But meanwhile, courtesy of the management, let's get the friendly process going with a touch of the champagnes all round. Are your glasses charged, gents and ladies?'

Veuve du Vernay corks popped and plastic cups

materialised as if from nowhere. Kangaroo Tours couriers moved smiling among the delayed holidaymakers.

'We may not be the youngest touring party to hit Aussie land this season,' Ficket said, raising a swilling tankard, 'but let's show 'em we can still put 'em down, or do I mean pull 'em down? – sorry, naughty, that one – down under! Ladies and gents, the toast is a hearty bon voyage to one and all!'

As the ex-Derbyshireman talked genially on, James began a discreet examination of his fellow tourists. Ficket's repeated reference to the age of the party were, if perhaps not altogether tactful, largely justified. In fact, James noted with a grim kind of satisfaction that a fair proportion of the Kangaroo travellers were older than himself. He recognised only one MCC member in the group – a panama-hatted skeleton who had last uttered coherent speech, if he remembered correctly, on the occasion of David Steele's dismissal after his plucky innings against Australia in the Lord's Test of the 1975 series. Next to him and his semi-conscious lady sat a cosier couple whose continuing intimacy was signalled not only by clasped hands but also by the fact that they were wearing identical binoculars and Free Forester blazers. James could not remember seeing either of them at Lord's.

At a distance from them had formed what appeared to be a group within a group. The womenfolk wore varieties of synthetic furs and the men echoed each other's taste for broad check suits that tended to swell around the ankles. There was another distinctive feature about this group – they were laughing loudly at Wally Ficket's jokes. James assumed they were Derbyshire members.

There were other faded faces that could have been

mistaken for any casual acquaintance made in a Torquay or Budleigh Salterton hotel lounge around this time of year save for the 'I'M FOLLOWING THE CRICKET WITH FICKET' labels that blazed on their hand luggage.

All this was only to be expected, James decided, bearing in mind that the significant administrators and correspondents were already in Australia; bearing in mind that younger people lacked the time and resources to undertake expeditions of this sort; bearing in mind, also, that cricket-loving VIPs would, unless absolutely necessary, have found a smoother way to get to Australia than at Kangaroo Tours cut prices. Everything, including the flight delay and Wally Ficket's gauche discourtesy to Jan, was to be expected – except perhaps for this middle-aged American tourist, with a face strangely resembling Rod Steiger's, weighted down by a plethora of photographic equipment and binoculars, but no wife. What was an American doing on a tour that claimed to be *following the cricket with Wally Ficket?*

2

The Balls were ushered to seats in the Jumbo's tail.

'I don't like to see what's happening,' said Jan, who had always been nervous of flying. 'On the other hand I'd be more terrified if I couldn't.' So she took the seat as well as James's hand in a tense rather than endearing grip. There remained a third seat on James's left and it was into this that the middle-aged American heaved. He was a big man, even when stripped of his safari load of photographic gear, and the capacious Jumbo seat seemedwholly inadequate for him and his equipment. Jan screamed softly as the Jumbo began to lumber towards take off and James sought to bury himself in the new Le Carré.

'Guess you're a ball fan too?'

'I beg your pardon?' James imagined some trans-Atlantic joke at his personal expense.

'Cricket!' the heavy American bawled against the roar of elephant-sized engines. 'I guess you're crazy about it, like me.'

'I think I'm going to be sick,' Jan said as the Jumbo suddenly thrust its nose skywards.

'In the bag, if I were you, darling,' James murmured.

'In the bag? Well I wouldn't be so sure,' the American voice clamoured at him over the lenses and light metres. 'I grant you Britishers have a pretty fine outfit down there. But remember what those guys did to you in the Bodyline games? – those Austies are always going to be hard to lick on their own home patch.'

In the bag provided, Jan was discreetly sick.

'You're going to ask what does a guy from New Jersey – Newark, New Jersey – know about cricket. I'll tell you: we've got a lot of blacks and Puerto Ricans who are playing the game back home now, and – funny thing – I got hooked. I guess I've read every copy of Wisdom since the year of Grace!'

'Get me some water,' Jan choked as the QANTAS Boeing banked southwards.

'Water!' James called.

'Walter – Walter Hammond, there was a player. But maybe that's kind of a sore spot with you fellas. That Walter Hammond sure handed it out to you limeys – he and Walter Woodfall!'

The professional in James could no longer be

persuaded to ignore this superficially demented American. He turned to search out the Rod Steiger face among the mounds of camera equipment and said innocently, 'That's very true; but then we always had Bradman.'

The American's stubby finger wagged. 'You don't catch me that easy. Sir Donald Badman played for South Australia, like the other doyen of Austie captains, Ian Church, right?'

'Ian Church? Surely you mean Ian Chappell.'

'You better make it a double brandy,' Jan moaned.

'Hey that could be the best idea this morning. Allow me to invite you two sweet people to join me in a toast – a toast to Mike Gatting and his British Cricketers!'

At least the American seemed to have influence with the cabin service. Three large brandies appeared as if by magic. Jan drained her glass at a swallow and fell immediately into a merciful sleep.

Meanwhile the American introduced himself. His name was Steve Burbek from, as he had already mentioned, Newark, New Jersey where he owned a hardware store. It evidently wasn't a big money-spinner. Burbek said he had cashed three years' hard savings in order to make this trip, which was surprising since he talked like a man who had only just scraped through a twenty-four-hour crash course in cricket lore and history.

'Yeah,' Burbeck mused over his plastic contained four-star, 'I guess we're going to be privileged to witness quite an epic combat for that Sheffield Shield. Personally I want to see how Alan Broader handles those bounders Bill Edmunds and Dick Grower. Those guys can certainly bang it around the park! Hey, but that's a helluva thing about those Ashes!' A

40

hand had suddenly thrust its way through the camera cases to grab James by his pinstripe sleeve. And now the heavy jowled face had become a formidable close up. 'Tell me who'd want to steal a thing like that?' Steve Burbeck demanded.

3

The Boeing powered out of the hot night like a liquid jet. As it shimmered towards the terminal buildings it presented a sleek illusion of refreshing sophistication, of tinkling ice in cognac glasses, of popping champagne corks and the swish of tonics on gin, of stockinged legs swung negligently over padded arm rests, of painted fingernails on the stems of exquisite glass. To the eyes of this man on the ground at Bahrain International Airport the Jumbo seemed as alluring as a mirage.

It was to be regretted, the man grimly reflected, that his orders permitted him no time for relaxation or indulgence on board this haven of sophistication. There would be work to do, hard, complex, dangerous work, from the moment he answered the stewardess's cordial 'Good evening, sir,' with an automatic pistol to her stomach.

It had been a long, tense wait in the dry departure lounge of Bahrain International Airport, and it was not yet over. The Jumbo's passengers were now de-planing, or those of them who had decided to sample the airport's non-alcoholic duty free wares or spend a penny in its ample urinals. And every second that passed seemed to increase the danger of a malfunction in the plan. A crucial mistiming on the part of the bribed official at the nose loader, perhaps. Or a too eager and too early show of aggression from the executive-suited Druse Militiaman who perspired beside him. Or the tell-tale disintegration of make-up on his own face, an oily substance designed to give him the complexion of a reasonably successful and unfanatical Middle Eastern businessman masking the natural and incriminating pallor of an underpaid agent of the KGB.

And behind all these tensions was the knowledge that there could be no failure on this mission, even though his still inadequately shaved accomplice was not of his choosing, even though he was but a pawn in a strategy devised at a mistily higher level. He knew that another failure would spell a fate far worse than permanent banishment to the hideous environment of the Russo-Chinese border.

So Agent I. Smirnov searched his breast pocket in a pretence of checking his boarding pass and ticket (he had been authorised no return) and sucked at a small flask concealed among his papers. Then he grimly wiped his mouth with the back of his hand as it was at last announced, in a babel of mis-pronounced tongues, that the QANTAS Boeing was ready for boarding.

From the terminal windows the Jumbo seemed to loom out of the hot darkness like a Gibraltar. The Russian's heart sank at the size of it.

One sweating Druse Militiaman at his side. Another unknown accomplice, boarded at London, somewhere among the forest of seats at the end of the nose loader. And with this they expected him to capture a castle.

A touch on his shoulder. The Russian raised his hands in an instinctive, almost relieved, gesture of surrender. Indeed it was a uniformed official who was stripping him of his shoulder bag, but as it happened he was a friend. As fast as Smirnov's reactions were slow, he was wrapping a duplicate shoulder bag around his neck. He felt the pressure of metal on his hip. At least the bribed official had done his job.

Smirnov entered the loader like a fox going reluctantly to earth. He was getting too old for this work, he reflected. Not old for love, not too old for the appreciation of civilised comforts, but old for danger and, yes far worse, too old to be continually running the risk of failure and its horrible consequences. Behind him he could hear the Druse Militiaman fiercely praying. He did not understand the Arabic words, but he had the unpleasant sensation that he was committing his soul to Allah.

The operation must have all the appearance of an everyday Middle Eastern hijack – these were his orders. If necessary, Jewish passengers were to be insulted, if not actually shot. American nationals were to be convincingly roughed-up without prejudicing the more cordial relationships which were currently developing between the two Superpowers.

However, the underlying purpose of the operation was to delay, perhaps terminally, the passage of the Englishman Ball to Australia. Yes, violently threatening, albeit imprecise, demands were to be issued for the release of various unspecified prisoners in Israeli and Egyptian gaols. The international media was to be urgently invited to the Beirut or Tripoli landing strip to see the pilot wriggling from a trembling revolver at his temple. And it was not beyond the mission's terms of reference that the Archbishop of Canterbury, or his special envoy, Terry Waite, should in due course be called in to mediate. But this much I. Smirnov knew for certain: unless the hijack

43

allowed two hours for the intensive interrogation of the Agent Ball, which, out of sight of the world's cameras would expose the true motive behind his Australian tour, the whole desperate plan would be accounted a failure.

'Good evening, Sir, I hope you enjoy your flight,' said the smiling QANTAS hostess.

'Can we start to kill now please?' the Druse Militiaman in an executive suit tensely enquired. Rather reluctantly, Smirnov began to grope in the exchanged bag for the crucial automatic pistol.

'Reinforcements at last!'

A strong arm was gripping him tightly around the shoulder and a large stomach was barrelling into his back, making it impossible for the Russian to get at the zip of his shoulder bag.

'Join us, friend, in a little illegal enterprise we've got going here.'

The man seemed to be putting him under arrest. Yet he called him 'friend' and talked of 'reinforcements' and 'illegal enterprises'. Was he the Security Officer, or the third agent Control had reported would have boarded the aircraft at Heathrow?

'We're trying to set up a record,' the man breathed spirituously into his ear. 'We want to be the first bunch of boozers to get officially pissed out of their minds in the heart of Saudi. I mean if I was to walk out of that door they would have my hand off, or even something more drastic – heh, heh, sorry, naughty one that. But as it is we're flying the flag, or should I say the Koala bear? Those wogs out there can't touch us. So long as we're kosher international travellers, we can commit bloody murder on the Michael Parkinson Express.'

The security officer, third agent or mere voluble

drunk conjured a plastic mug out of the air and filled it with whisky with a duty-free largesse. 'Join us, friend, in a toast to the land of the amber liquid,' he commanded, 'in the amber liquid of cousin Jock.'

The situation was confusing and frightening. In the circumstances I. Smirnov needed little encouragement to drink. However the large man had got his arms pinioned in an apparently fraternal grip, while behind him the Druse Militiaman was tugging at his shoulder bag in order to help himself to the weapons and explosives.

'Drink up, friend. Here's to you, Sambo!' Wally Ficket, ex of Derbyshire and England, genially toasted. 'Seriously, no reflection on the colour of your skin, nor your mate's either. Believe me we've had duskier in the Derbyshire eleven! No kidding, it's a pleasure and an honour to welcome you two aboard. Frankly they've landed me with a right lot of geriatrics on this jaunt – present company excepted of course.' The former batsman/wicketkeeper nodded towards a posse of flushed faces belonging to the segment of the party James Ball had mentally identified as Derbyshire members. 'Meet the lads. As for the rest of the bunch, I can promise you there's not a laugh in them. So far, we've seen as much action elbow-wise as a TT convention. But then I suppose most of the old dears are travelling without livers. Or should I say prostates? Sorry, naughty one that!'

'Pass me please the weapons and I will kill him,' the Druse Militiaman hissed in Smirnov's ear.

Like convenient heart markers, three silver lions decorated his friend's (or assailant's) bulging jacket. Smirnov knew from hard-won experience that he was in the presence of the coveted blazer of England, as much as symbol of English traditionalism as a guardsman's bearskin or a City of London stockbroker's pinstripe suit. Cricket was England's noblest game; and it was also, he understood, a notorious front for the British Secret Services; but it was common knowledge that Britain's security services were deeply penetrated by the KGB, so it was a reasonable hypothesis that this apparent cricketer was his awaited accomplice.

The man clearly wished to pass as a Test Match performer, and yet he appeared badly out of training and shape. In fact, the more I. Smirnov reflected on the matter – a process accelerated by the tugs of strangulation intensity the Militiaman was making on his shoulder bag – the more he was inclined to the conviction that this was the third agent, and that the disjointed phrases the man was mouthing were code words which Control had omitted to pass on. Put him, before it is too late, to the test:

'The weather I trust is amiable in London?' Smirnov suggested with a conspiratorial wink. 'You know I have been to London on many important businesses such as we are undertaking now. I have many dear friends in London, also including among your elite Test Match cricketers. I know, similarly, that the coveted England blazer can be a convenient cover for those of us who have Party work to do. It is a pleasure to meet you, comrade; but I do not believe you earn those lions on the cricketing field. Am I guessing your secret?'

'What are you saying Sambo?' the big, genial man was suddenly not so friendly.

'Only that you could be a good comrade, but not so good a Test batterman, not so good at the balls.' I. Smirnov raised the plastic glass of whisky in a friendly toast leading to a hearty swig.

The chubby face was purpling. 'Look, woppo, I grafted an innings at that Headingley Test. I don't care what the frigging score card says – those ten runs could have been worth their weight in gold if anybody had been able to stay with me. Yes, if you want to make something of it you could say I could have pushed the scoring rate along a bit; what you don't know is that I was batting to orders, chum! My orders were to keep up the end. If you're insinuating I let England down, I'm going to have a serious disagreement with you. Why the hell do you think they dropped me from the next Test? I'll tell you, Sambo, if you haven't got the brains to work it out: it was because I was too fucking good – are you receiving me, Darky? Too good to keep my place with that bunch of spankers, because my defensive technique was putting the lot of them to shame. And yet you walk in here with the bloody effrontery to suggest that Wally Ficket hasn't earned his England Cap. Now you're needling me, Mohammed!'

A lot of things began to happen very fast. The first was an explosive hook to the jaw from the outraged batsman/wicketkeeper. Conviviality had, however, slowed the Derby man's fist just sufficiently to allow Smirnov to duck under it. In so doing he enabled the Druse Militiaman to wrench the bag from his shoulder and delve, panting, into its mixed contents of automatic firepower, grenades and plastic explosives.

For some time distraught air hostesses had been fruitlessly urging the party to take their seats as the plane was on the point of take off. Now they were reinforced by muscle. Two burly Australian cabin stewards crashed into the gathering, disarmed Ficket of his slopping drink, hoisted him into a vacant seat and snapped a safety belt on him. Smirnov was similarly roughly handled. Before he quite realised it, he was laced into a window seat on the far side of Ficket.

'*Liberazion!*' screamed the Druse Militiaman, swivelling the shoulder bag, sub-machine-gun wise, around the heads of the passengers. One steward lifted him, struggling, into a seat across the gangway. The other grabbed the shoulder bag and slammed it into an overhead locker.

'Gentlemen, you will kindly remain in your seats and refrain from smoking or drinking until we are safely airborne,' the senior steward warned.

Just another routine Jumbo taking off into the desert night. But in an overhead locker nestled a piece of luggage that could turn the flight into a nightmare.

4

The sun was setting on the Adelaide Oval. The players had left the field. The ground was now completely empty – it had been far from filled all day. In the roseate towers of Adelaide Cathedral a bell was tolling for evening service, or perhaps for the sanctity of conventional cricket.

Sebastian Gover sat with a gin and tonic in the press box re-reading with bitter sweet emotions his first despatch, already telexed to London, for a major quality newspaper. It had been a red-letter day in the life of a formidable new writing talent, but not for cricket itself. Powerful imagery and exciting metaphors had had to come to the rescue of a day that had been obstinately short of stroke play and incident. It was ironical, Sebastian Gover reflected with a little sadness and some pleasure, but this day was going to be more enjoyable to read about than to have witnessed, especially for those readers able, for the price of an *Observer*, to borrow his imaginative and life-enhancing binoculars.

Indeed, the young reporter decided with a wry smile playing at the rim of his gin and tonic, probably the only hope this day at Adelaide had of surviving into posterity was as a piece by Sebastian Gover in a volume of his collected writings or in an anthology dedicated to the craft of Cardus, Gover, Arlott and Ross.

He took another sip of his drink – it tasted sweeter now – and then again re-read his last redolent, some might say Mozartian, closing paragraphs:

The naked scorecard reads South Australia 195 for 5 wickets. Impressions can be disconcerting when one brutally strips a day's play of its richly brocaded pattern of high hopes and small failures, of artful field placings and elaborate, if futile, appeals. The bare body revealed in this case is certainly no Rubens or Renoir nude. The day in its frankest outline is not such as to draw a gasp of admiration from the connoisseur of cricket's more gorgeous contours. At the same time it would be a serious error of judgement, and indeed of taste, to ignore the garments in which this final score at Adelaide has been clad.

There has been much minor detail to savour in South Australia's dogged occupation of the crease, and much to approve in MCC's strenuous efforts to make a starker impression on a humid afternoon in Adelaide. In particular, the chauvinist that lurks in all our souls will have been heartened by the bowling of Brian Philpott, the long-hoped-for redeemer of England's languishing pace aspirations. Just before tea, the young Warwickshire thundercloud found a dart which demolished Hookes's castle like a second Troy. And the appeal which he directed to the heavens for a

49

caught behind off Sleep must have earned the concurrence of Jove, if not of Umpire Cronin.

We shall see more and hear more of Brian Philpott in other more crowded arenas, and if the gods are indulgent enough to provide him with a more responsive wicket we shall see even more illustrious castles than that of D. Hookes' crumble to his chariot of fire.

Sebastian Gover felt a hand on his shoulder. It wasn't an approving god, but it wasn't an ordinary mortal either. Gover was looking up into the creased, tanned face of Ray Hammerton of the Melbourne *Argus*, doyen of Australian cricket correspondents.

'It's your first day in the spotlight, isn't it, son? How d'yer make out?' the great man kindly enquired. With a mixture of hesitation and pride, Sebastian raised his article in an offering.

'Yes,' said the journalist, professionally skimming through the close-set typed pages to the final paragraph, 'that's a tidy piece of writing. "The young Warwickshire thundercloud" – yes that's nice. Your editor should be able to make something of that. Shame about Philpott, isn't it?'

'What about Philpott?' Gover hesitantly wondered.

'Haven't you heard? It's today's big story – today's only story. Surprised your colleagues didn't tell you. Your young Warwickshire thundercloud has signed with Ernie Tyburn's mob. I'm afraid your poms will have to do without a genuine quickie for a while longer. If I were you, son, I'd get back to my editor. You could maybe catch the later editions, if you're lucky.'

Sleepers

James Ball had fallen asleep. Awake he might have felt guilty for doing so, for he had snoozed off over the second chapter of the new Le Carré George Smiley adventure. It was, of course, no secret in Whitehall circles that Le Carré's master creation was to a large extent based on the career and personality of James himself. Even in his slumber James was conscious of committing an act of ingratitude, although its nature for the time being eluded him.

In another sense – assuming he had still been functioning with all his senses – James had reason to be grateful for slumber. The James Bond adventure, twitching in faded Technicolor in the inflight screen, had not ceased to irritate him, despite the fact he had pointedly refused to pay for headphones, with its grotesque misrepresentation of the whole ethos and practice of secret service life. Sleep had rescued him, not before time, from Roger Moore's latest tasteless travesty, as it had from the oppressive conversation of the cricket enthusiast from Newark, New Jersey. James was therefore unconscious of the plaintive but insistent voice which was now issuing from the row of seats behind him.

'The score from Adelaide. I wish to know how Mr Gatting and co are faring against South Australia.'

He was not to see the panama-hatted half-skeleton of an MCC member, whose last recollected utterance

51

had been at the Lord's Test of 1975, rise with difficulty to his feet to begin a stick-propelled march down the aisle, nor hear him bleat, 'Stewardess, you are an Australian are you not? It is your duty to be informed of the score!'

Certainly James had no way of comprehending the mental and emotional turmoil that was stirring under the slightly fraying panama hat. For this venerable man (according to the records, the fourth most senior living MCC member), life had finally presented him with the opportunity to make a meaningful contribution. The call had been a long time in coming. In fact, it had been impatiently awaited since the summer of 1936 when the harsh winds from Spain had overnight converted a convinced Lloyd George liberal into a fully committed enemy of Fascism.

He had expected that the Party would post him immediately, in spite of his age (he was not far off forty then), to an International Brigade on the Madrid front. At that time he was publishing verse fairly regularly in his family's Gloucestershire parish magazine (an uncle was the Bishop of Bristol) and he had half fancied a romantic death in the olive groves in the manner of the young poet John Cornford, although he wrote in the manner of Sir John Square and was at least ten years older. But the Party had said, 'No, Percy Gwynne-Watson (for this was the elderly man's name), you are an aristocrat, a member of England's influential elite, educated at Winchester and Trinity College, Cambridge; your contacts are too valuable for us to risk you in what may prove to be only the first skirmish in a world class struggle. You will be of more use to us if you continue, for the time being, to appear to lead the indolent life of a typical capitalist jackal of leisure.'

'But there must be something more I can do for the Party!' Gwynne-Watson had pleaded some months later, walking on the Sussex Downs above Chichester with his controller, a timber exporter from Riga.

'Yes, the Party would approve if you were to take up an appointment with your elite Foreign Office.'

'I'm afraid I flunked my exams with the FO when I came down from Cambridge and now I'm over the age limit,' the younger Gwynne-Watson had blushed.

'Then you should secure a post with the MI5 subsidiary. We understand the required qualifications are considerably less demanding. Besides your family will have influence.'

'I'm afraid I've blotted my copy-book there too,' Gwynne-Watson had confessed. 'I was seen from the Dorchester leading the Jarrow marchers down Park Lane. The powers that be are never going to forget that, even though I only joined them at Watford. Still, there must be something I can do?'

'We will need to consider the problem,' his controller had answered with a wave before vanishing down a lane in the direction of Petworth.

His final instructions had been handed to him in a folded copy of the *Tatler* on a windswept Chorley Wood Common six months later. In essence they stipulated that since he seemed unable to find permanent employment in sensitive areas, and yet enjoyed the benefit of a reasonable private income, he should lose no time in inserting himself into London's exclusive 'clubland' where it was well known that the nation's administrators chose to spend their leisure hours. One club, in particular, was recommended to him for regular attendance – the Marylebone Cricket Club, or as it was familiarly dubbed, 'the Lords', because of its intimate associations with the English Parliament's Upper House.

Percy Gwynne-Watson had always disliked cricket, had indeed often been brutally thrashed at his prep school for absence from compulsory matches. But he was a loyal agent of the USSR. From 1938 to the recent season, with a brief interruption for wartime service with an Ack-Ack battery in Dumfries, he had not failed to attend the first three days of every Test match played at Lord's, plus every Middlesex v Sussex Whitsun match.

From time to time, acting on the nod from a pavilion door-keeper, hopeful young cricket chroniclers would approach Percy Gwynne-Watson with the aim of tapping his almost unique reservoir of spectator experience. They would always be brushed aside out of what they supposed was eccentricity or the arrogance of age but what was in reality ignorance. For Percy Gwynne-Watson had dozed off through an extraordinary number of historic innings.

He had, for instance, slept through all 240 historic runs made by W. R. Hammond during his legendary onslaught on the Australian paceman E. R. McCormick in the Lord's Test of 1938. Bradman's last blistering fling at headquarters in Australia's 1948 tour again had caught him napping, though he had woken up in time to see him neatly taken at slip by Edrich off Bedser. Len Hutton's masterly 145 against a rampant Lindwall and Miller in the Coronation Year Test had of necessity been a slow business, but Gwynne-Watson had been able to pass the time between sleep and a volume of *Das Kapital*, secreted under his scorecard. He had dozed through the entirety of E. R. Dexter's thrilling counter-attack on Hall and Griffith in the 1963 West Indies Test, but in fairness this

54

innings had been as short as it was spectacular and had caught a good few other MCC members not fully roused from their overnight slumber.

Veteran Lord's goers will always argue whether this Dexter innings or Colin Milburn's extraordinary battering of the 1968 Australians takes the palm of post-war Test batting excellence at Lord's, at least before the advent of Botham. Others will advance the claims of Greg Chappell's dazzling 131 in 'Massie's Match' in 1972, Colin Cowdrey's slightly stolider demolition of Ramadhin and Valentine in 1956 and of course, for sheer pluck, that 50 by David Steele of Northants against the fury of Lillee and Thomson in 1975. Others again will point to memorable contributions from Tony Grieg, Richard Benaud, T. W. Graveney, P. B. H. May, Garfield Sobers, and, of course, Ian Botham. Percy Gwynne-Watson had no clear favourite since he retained no clear recollection of any of these epic knocks.

It sometimes occured to Percy Gwynne-Watson, especially as he grew older, how much more profitably all this Test-going time could have been spent. Even in his eighties he could guarantee to stay wide awake through any Saturday matinee performance of *Tosca* or *La Bohème* or an afternoon TV presentation of a vintage Hollywood musical such as *Top Hat* or *Gold Diggers of 1932*.

Yet the Party demanded that personal inclination should be subordinated to the cause, and Gwynne-Watson selflessly obeyed. True, he had been slow to cultivate the influential and fruitful contacts that were expected of him, but then since prep school Gwynne-Watson had never found it easy to make friends. He had, after all, joined the Party to see battle, not to discuss generations of fragile England batting orders with rural deans and retired civil servants. All the same, he had managed over the years to establish the persona of something of an authority on the game, albeit a none too approachable one. At a distance his fitful snorts and snores had been taken as expressions of Augustan disapproval of sloppy modern tendencies. James Ball, for instance, had assumed that his outburst on the occasion of David Steele's dismissal in the 1975 Test had been a cry of disgust at a man who could get himself out so soon after a maiden Test half-century. In fact his wrath had been directed at the wildly cheering crowd for waking him from yet another merciful shuteye.

Now the waiting was over. When he had almost despaired of ever seeing active service for Communism, a midnight call had ordered him to report immediately with his compliant wife to Heathrow in his full MCC regalia prior to boarding for Australia. Objective: the hijacking of a QANTAS passenger aircraft. Should he travel armed? No, the necessary weaponry and armaments experts would be introduced at Bahrain. His role was to create a sufficient diversion to enable the trained operatives to gain effective control of the aircraft. Orders received and understood! The third agent, boarded at Heathrow as promised to I. Smirnov, was moving grimly into action.

James Ball, who had seldom if ever slept through an England–Australia Test, was still unconscious of the turn events were taking in this even deadlier crisis. He was not to see the scuffle turning to a struggle that was developing between the Soviet mole Gwynne-Watson and a pair of QANTAS hostesses only a few rows from him, nor was he to hear the piercing screams the elderly spy was now emitting.

'Young women, your brochure gave me clearly to understand that this flight has been reserved exclusively for devotees of English cricket! In the circumstances, I take your refusal to furnish me with the close of play score from Adelaide not only as the height of discourtesy but as a palpable breach of contract. If you tell me that this aeroplane is not in wireless contact with Australia, I shall tell you that you are two lying boobies! I warn you, vixens, if you are unable to give me satisfaction I shall insist on talking directly to the Captain and his wireless operator!'

James Ball was still asleep when the agent, supporting himself on one stewardess's shoulder, brought his walking stick savagely down on the other's head and with a side swipe at the remaining obstacle freed himself for a shuffling dash towards the stairs and the cockpit. The burly steward who blocked his way was not expecting the brutal poke to the groin that felled him; he had imagined, after all, that he was confronting an elderly gentleman belonging to the MCC. There was nothing gentlemanly in the manner in which Gwynne-Watson toe-capped his writhing body aside and finally gained the first step of the stairs that led to First Class and the *controls*.

'*Arriba!*' he jubilantly piped as he mounted upwards '*Abajo los falangistas! Ne Passeran!* We have nothing to lose but our chains!'

They are crazy to permit old English aristocrats aboard such expensive aircraft, the Agent I. Smirnov thought to himself as he sat wedged against the window by the now slumberous bulk of Wally Ficket ex of Derbyshire and England.

The Druse Militiaman across the gangway was faster to recognise that a unique opportunity had been created. Delaying only to tear off his businessman's tie, he leapt to his feet, ripped the shoulder bag out of the overhead locker, pulled out a Kalashnikov rifle and raced towards the stairs.

James Ball was not to hear the fanatical cry with which he clipped the MCC's fourth most senior member to the floor and drew himself up for a spring at the men at the controls.

'Death to all Jewish pig and Shi'ite pro-Jewish extremists. Death to Reagan US imperialist Jewish sympathisers. Liberazion!'

James was conscious only of a vague stirring to his left as the American cricket enthusiast from Newark, New Jersey, rose cumbrously to his feet and, selecting a telescopic-lensed Nikon camera from his plethora of photographic equipment, riddled the Druse Militiaman with what was in effect an automatic weapon fitted with a silencer.

It was the voice of the Captain that finally roused James and, incidentally, woke Jan. The intercom tone was superficially calm, but Ball had a trained ear for the hint of anxiety that could often underlie bland official statements.

'We've had just a little bit of a barney downstairs, as some of you may have noticed. We're back to normal now and our cabin service will be coming round shortly with a late evening snack and refreshments from the bar. Meanwhile my co-pilot and I are checking the controls here just to ensure that no serious damage has been done. Basically everything looks to be in full functioning order; but we are just a little curious about this little pellet that seems to be lodged in our landing gear controls. It's not anything to worry about seriously because we've already got one set of wheels responding and we are in direct radio contact with Colombo, only a few hundred miles ahead of us now, and they've agreed to lay on special landing facilities, should they be necessary.

'Meanwhile we're going down to just a few thousand feet above sea level just to ensure we don't put too much of a strain on our compression system. You'll feel a bit of a jolt, perhaps just a spot of nausea, but you can rest assured we're making a perfectly controlled descent. . . .'

'My God,' cried Jan, 'we're sinking!'

'This isn't a boat, darling,' James gently reminded her.

'If only it *was!*' Jan unashamedly screamed. 'At least a boat has bloody lifeboats!'

James put his arm round his wife's heaving shoulders and gently reminded her that QANTAS pilots were acknowledged as being some of the most reliable in the business.

Privately he prepared to meet his Maker, but the smoke issuing from Burbek's Nikon lens distracted him. He had never seen a camera overheat like that.

Down Under

'The High Commissioner was worried about you,' revealed Sandy Winchester in the arrivals hall of Sydney Airport.

'We were a little concerned for ourselves,' James admitted. 'But how very kind of the High Commissioner to have us met, particularly by an old friend like you.'

'Quite a bumpy landing at Colombo, we were given to understand,' Sandy said.

'I feel you should try to find a place for our Australian pilot in the New Year's Honours, Sandy. I am not technically minded as you know, but I think we may have established a record for landing with the minimum of undercarriage.'

'Still you're both looking extremely well,' lied the seasoned diplomat who had worked with James as a young man on the Balkans Desk at a time when his Majesty's Government was supporting several violently opposed partisan groups. 'Jan, you're looking as gorgeous as ever!'

In fact, the couple were looking badly shaken by their experience. Jan, ashen-faced, was wearing a pair of dark glasses to protect her from a searing headache. James seemed strangely shrunken and even older than his years, which Sandy was in a position to know were many. This worried the diplomat, because information had been reaching the High Commission's office in Canberra, from far too many embassy back doors to be lightly dismissed, to the effect that James Ball was not altogether *persona grata* in Australia. Indeed, for reasons the Commission's security people had so far been unable to untangle, his life could actually be in danger. Ball himself may or may not have noted the extra pressure of protectiveness from the hand that was guiding him to the waiting limousine.

Outside in the even glare of the Australian sun, Wally Ficket was explaining to the rest of the Kangaroo party that a coach would be arriving shortly to take them to their hotel.

'I think I'd sell my pearls not to travel in that coach, assuming it ever arrives,' Jan murmured.

'But as it is, darling, we have a chauffeur-driven saloon,' James said loudly as a token of appreciation for his old friend's courtesy. 'A Cadillac!' he exclaimed when, relieved at last of their luggage, the couple had settled in the plush back seat. 'In my day it was always a Daimler.'

'The English aren't too popular out here at the moment,' Sandy Winchester leaned over from the front passenger seat to confide. 'For the time being we find it expedient not to parade the home-made product.'

'Really?' A grey eyebrow cocked.

'I tell you one thing, James, there's going to be all hell to pay if we thrash them again in the Tests. You see, the Australian *amour propre* has been taking a bit of a beating lately. We don't want to be unpatriotic, but frankly, some of us at the High Commission are praying we lose the Ashes, the mythical ones, I mean. Incidentally that's a rotten business about the Urn at

Lord's. I'm afraid it's created a lot of bad feeling out here.'

'Are there any circumstances in which one wishes to present the old enemy with the proudest prize in sport?' James asked sternly. 'As for the theft of the Lord's Urn, I fail to see how that can create bad feelings here. We are surely the injured party.'

He turned to look glumly at the posters and the buildings flashing past. He noted a dominance of the car-park school of architecture that had done so much to disfigure the outskirts of London. He thought this could be the M4 from Heathrow on a particularly arid August day.

'There has been rather too much injudicious comment and speculation in the London press which, of course, has been quoted verbatim out here.' Sandy Winchester patted his sleekly combed hair, the colour of which gave him his name. 'What is deeply resented is the implication that an Australian is responsible, although at the same time your average "cobber" believes passionately that the Urn rightly belongs here.'

'Or in Melbourne?' James suggested with only the hint of a smile.

'Yes, indeed. Things haven't been helped by the clear insinuations in our yellow press that Ernie Tyburn is Suspect Number One. Now Master Tyburn isn't everyone's cup of tea by any means. The Australian Cricket Board would dearly like to see him back in the scrap metal business where he came from. But he *is* respected – your average "cobber" has a lot of time for the successful self-made man, however unrefined his methods of doing business. And of course, he has attracted a lot of support with his demand for the return of the Urn to these shores.

That's why these frankly irresponsible innuendos from the gutter end of Fleet Street couldn't be more unfortunate.'

Perhaps it hadn't been at the Balkan Desk that he had last worked with Winchester. Perhaps after all, James decided, it had been at the Nazi German Desk in the Appeasement period.

'Mind you, there's been a certain amount of wild speculation in the Australian papers too. Some of it about you, James, as it happens.' Winchester turned in his seat again to submit the doyen of the security world to a searching gaze. His mouth was wearing a smile, but it did not hide the anxiety in the diplomat's eyes. 'The rumour being reported is that you're not strictly here on pleasure – in fact, that your arrival is not unconnected with the theft of the Urn. I don't suppose there's a word of truth in it, is there James?'

'I will repeat the statement I made at Colombo, Sandy,' James sighed, 'where I was held by some obviously overheated foreign correspondents to be the unwitting cause of the dramatic events we experienced over the Bay of Bengal. I am *retired* from the Service and I am here on *holiday* to watch the cricket. End of statement.'

'I'll tell the High Commissioner,' Sandy Winchester said with a more genuine smile. 'I know he'll be reassured. As I've hinted, the other situation is a little delicate out here at the moment. Passions are running a big high. We're all at full stretch trying to dampen things down. Trying to keep a weather eye out for your safety could break the camel's back, as it were; I mean if you *had* come here on business.'

They were in a Cadillac, but it was moving at a diplomatically modest speed. James had noticed that they had been overtaken by a Datsun and an imported

Citroën Diane. Now a cumbersome beer truck swung raucously in front of the High Commission's car and then abruptly braked. Suddenly the road ahead was a death trap of crates labelled 'Castlemaine XXXX'.

The Cadillac's steady 28 m.p.h. enabled the chauffeur to brake effectively enough to halt the car inches short of the deadly lager; but in so doing he had pushed the Cadillac into a swerve that brought the car's flashy rear end into the overtaking lane.

'I can't stand this God-awful holiday!' screamed Jan as a Jaguar smashed into the exposed metalwork. 'It's becoming a perfect nightmare!' she added shrilly as a speeding Buick impacted with the interlocked Jaguar.

'Is everyone all right?' Sandy Winchester called when the cacophony of violence of metal on metal had finally ceased.

James ran a swift hand over his person. No blood. No stab of pain which would have been the instant signal of broken bones. Next to him Jan was weeping. A reassuring sign. Concussion or even major fractures seldom produced as simple a reaction as tears.

'I think we can say we have survived Mr Border's opening attack,' he gamely responded with a nod towards the picture of the Australian Test Captain and Castlemaine sponsor that decorated the back of the beer truck.

'Well,' Sandy Winchester slightly brightened, 'I suppose it's just as well your hotel is on the outskirts of Sydney. At a pinch we could probably walk it from here.'

He tried not to look too relieved at the sound of the police siren's wail, because he would have betrayed the real anxiety he was beginning to feel for his old superior's safety. The fact was that he had not come completely clean with James. The High Commission still operated Daimlers. The Cadillac had been hired at the High Commissioner's express direction in order not to advertise the arrival of the top security man in Australia.

And yet those Castlemaine crates had been dropped in their path with the precision of a daylight bomber. At whose orders? Sandy Winchester hardly dared to guess.

'As long as no bones are broken,' he smiled into the back seat of a half demolished Cadillac.

Mega Morning

1

'I hope you all slept well,' said Wally Ficket. 'I know I did, but that's maybe because I've left my good lady at home. Sorry, naughty one that! Anyhow, I'd suggest we take things easy today. You could catch the fourth day of the New South Wales v Tasmania game, but for my money your time would be better spent getting acclimatised and seeing the sights. So why not have a look at that bridge, take in that Opera House? I can't promise you Joan Collins because it isn't a Soap Opera House! Sorry about that. Or you could take a bus out to Bondi, ladies, and get yourself a gorgeous man. What am I saying? I meant a gorgeous tan!'

Their guide was addressing them in the breakfast room of the Ned Kelly, an out-of-town hotel which had not, after all, lived up to the Balls' worst fears. Dinner, after a fraught day of collision and late arrival by police patrol car, had been hot and digestible, even if the steak portions had been excessive, and they had been able to wash it down with an acceptable South Australian claret. The beds had been aired, the sheets had been clean and – apart from a lamentable absence of Oxford marmalade – breakfast had been no severer hardship than might be undergone at any comparable English hotel feeding one of the major motorways.

There were other encouraging omens. The embarrassing cricket enthusiast from Newark, New Jersey, had not rejoined the party after Colombo. James would not be pestered by any more of his inane cricket comments, nor nagged by the suspicion that he dealt in more sinister hardware than hammers and nails. Again, the noisy Derbyshire members and their no longer fur-coated wives appeared to have been gratifyingly sobered by the baffling series of events over the Bay of Bengal.

In this connection, James noted that the skeletal old MCC member was still wearing bandages under his panama hat. James was not the only one to have been unconscious of the efforts Percy Gwynne-Watson had made to assist in the hijack. In fact, his one-man demonstration had been largely forgotten due to the greater dramas that were to follow. He had been treated as a victim of the outrage in the Colombo hospital where a severely wounded Druse Militiaman lay closely guarded in intensive care.

Now he looked out on the world from under his head bandages with a fiercer gleam in his eyes. After decades of waiting, Percy Gwynne-Watson had won his first scars in the class struggle. For him the battle had only just begun.

'Now after supper I've got a little surprise for you all,' Wally Ficket revealed. 'My spies inform me the lads will be flying in from Adelaide tonight and putting up at the Sydney Hilton, and if I know the lads they are going to have worked up a respectable thirst on that flight. So I suggest we all call down at the Hilton bar later and mingle. My hunch is we'll find the New South Wales lads have dropped in to welcome them. You could find yourself rubbing shoulders with exciting Test prospects like "Digger"

Dyson, "Mattress" Matthews, "Dusty" Beard and "Chuck" Skilbeck.'

There was a mild buzz of excitement among the geriatric cricket fans. Wally raised a pair of fleshy wicketkeeper's hands in an appeal for silence.

'I don't think it's going to be a fancy dress occasion at this stage of the tour. But if you've got a fez or a solar topee or any kind of funny hat, it could help the socialising. One word of advice to the ladies, don't dress too formal. We modern England cricketers are a pretty laid-back bunch, as you'll discover if you play your cards right. Take "Goldie" – that's the team's laughing but affectionate sobriquet for "Davo" Gower – he may have been to a posh school and all that, but I've never seen him in a tie, let alone tails. So it's slacks and sandals, ladies, and if you're really looking for a little movement off the wicket a nice exposure of midriff never goes amiss. And I don't mean Denis Amiss! Sorry about that. I warn you, you're going to have competition from the "Sheilas"; but now's the time to make your pitch before Fran Edmonds, Gelda Gatting, Mary Lamb, and the rest of the wives fly out. Sorry, naughty one that. . . .'

'When *are* the wives supposed to be flying out?' Jan wondered, affecting almost complete indifference. For his part, James knew only too well that her studied indifference could often mask a keen interest.

'I haven't the slightest idea, my darling, and I don't think it really need concern you, need it? Personally I don't follow the domestic lives of the England crick-eters, but I'm pretty sure Mrs Gatting isn't called Gelda.'

'I always think he has such sweet, innocent eyes – like a little boy looking for a mother,' Jan said ominously.

James Ball shoved through the swing doors of the
Ned Kelly into the dust-blown Australian suburban
summer morning. I will not, he said to himself,
subject myself to Ficket's ludicrous and demeaning
bromides. I shall go where the heart listeth.

'Cab!' he called at the passing traffic of trucks,
late commuters and housewives with children late for
school.

The hotel commissioner said that James was lucky
to attract one, so far out of the city centre. Ball hardly
acknowledged him and certainly declined to tip him
as he bundled into the back of the cream coloured
Volvo. For the Englishman had been seized by an
ecstatic mood, a recurring frenzy as old as his earliest
schooldays.

'To the cricket!' he commanded the driver as a
smile of uncontrolled glee eclipsed an aging face's
moonscape.

Hundreds, perhaps thousands of times, he had
issued a similar command to a London taxi driver.
But never before in Australia, least of all in the capital
of mighty New South Wales. And so, for all his years,
he had really only seen the half of it. He had decades
of catching up to do.

Somewhere down this street called Harris (by any
chance after the Lord and master strokesman of
Kent?) lay the youth of Victor Trumper, Sidney
Gregory, Warren Bardsley, poor Young Archie
Jackson, Sir Donald Bradman, Stan McCabe and the
swashbuckling RAAF flyer Keith Miller. And somewhere not too distant – though it was difficult to
imagine in this Americanised thoroughfare – lay half
the achievements of Hobbs and Hammond, the high

69

noon of Larwood and Voce and the full flowering of MacLaren, 'Ranji' and A. E. Stoddart.

They said the ball came truer and faster off Australian turf. As a result the class batsman had more encouragement to play his strokes than in the seamier climate of England. So perhaps only at a ground like Sydney would it have been possible to see the great blades swung in the most perfect symmetry. It might be the last day of a mundane New South Wales v Tasmania match, but James was impatient to sniff the historic turf and open his sensory perceptions to the golden ghosts who batted eternally in the great arena under a legendary Hill.

'What do we know of cricket who only England know?' he found himself, to his slight surprise, demanding of the driver.

'I'm an Australian rules football fan myself,' the man answered taciturnly.

It was not what the photographs had led him to expect. The photographs suggested a kind of Edwardian elegance, a certain stateliness and formality. (Wasn't it Denis Compton who had once had to vault the turnstile here because he had no papers to prove that he was England's number four batsman?) The gate at which the taxi driver was depositing him looked functional to say the least; no hint along this concrete wall of the elegance of Sydney's renowned pavilion and ladies' stand. James reminded himself, however, that Australians share with the Americans a lack of proper respect for the past and a craving for the new and the unsightly. In a new country, he told himself, you can never hope to find things quite as you had envisaged. These reflections were swept away by an enormous crowd roar.

'My goodness, a wicket must have fallen!' James cried like a twelve-year-old, and was only prevented by a garishly uniformed official from vaulting the turnstile like Denis Compton.

He surfaced panting in a crowded stand in time to see the jubilant celebrations that were still marking the fall of the last wicket. Aloft on the bare shoulders of a team of giggling hostesses the bowler was gulping at a magnum of champagne. The wicket-keeper was dancing for joy in the company of an Eurasian belly-dancer while the fielders had gleefully crowded around another scantily-clad – could that conceivably be a brassiere she was holding on high?

Meanwhile the departing batsman, a downcast figure in luminous plastic armour, was being escorted up the pavilion steps by Donald Duck and Goofy.

James was too stunned, and in any case too short-sighted, to fully comprehend the scene. But an explanation was soon provided.

'Give him a big hand gentlemen and ladies!' erupted the ground's lavish public address system. 'He's making his debut in MEGATEST cricket and already he's taken three wickets for five thousand dollars! Yes, let's say a big hello and "well paid, sir!" to Brian Philpott, the English quickie with the mean inswinger who, like thousands of today's top international stars, has decided there's a more rewarding future in MEGATESTS!

'And hasn't that proved a prudent decision for Brian? With three top South African rebel scalps to his credit, he's bowled his way into big money with a thousand dollars per wicket. Plus that tempting two thousand bonus that's automatically awarded to every bowler who takes three wickets on his maiden appearance in MEGATESTS!

Shocked and disoriented, James Ball raised his binoculars and searched the scoreboard. He found an illuminated display ablaze with figures. With difficulty he made out the following information:

Steve McGlew lbw Philpott minus	$Aus	500.00
Total earnings	$Aus	43,700.00
Garth Smuts c Watts b Philpott plus	$Aus	2,000.00
Total earnings	$Aus	177,000.00
Vic van Rynveld cb Philpott minus	$Aus	1,000.00
Total earnings minus	$Aus	51,370.00

'But this could be just the start of the big payout for England's Brian Philpott on his maiden MEGATEST!' bawled the public address system. 'One more wicket and Brian's in the "double your money" league with a chance to earn a princely two thousand dollars per wicket, plus debut bonus and a selection of fabulous leisure prizes courtesy of the Ernie Tyburn Trust! Spare a little sympathy for his last victim, Vic van Rynveld. While Brian soars in the earnings aggregates, poor Vic seems to have lost that golden touch. Minus 51,370 dollars? Better wear your pads when you see your bank manager tomorrow, Vic!

'But this is Brian's day, and the way he's bowling now suggests to ex-Australian Test star Rick Craig, who's sitting beside me here, that he could blast his way into the coveted "five wickets plus" jackpot reward scale. And that could mean an incredible four thousand dollars per wicket payout and massive double-up in the value of his Ernie Tyburn Trust leisure prize selection. *And*, if he can answer a few simple questions on showbiz subjects, a chance to compete in the MEGATEST "Winner-Takes-All" single wicket knock-out final which, as you know, could earn him the opportunity to be the escort at the Tyburn

Leisure Complex of his choice of the Australian cinema's brightest and most bewitching star – the super sex-goddess from Queensland, the one and only, the adorable Charlene!'

James's binoculars were shaking from an admixture of their owner's state of confusion and disbelief. When he finally managed to steady them, he found they were trained not on the crazy statistics of the score-board but on the gilded spectators seated in a splendid box evocative of quite other games, notably in Imperial Rome.

The box was draped in bunting and stacked with flowers and glittering femininity. From a bevy of sequined handmaidens a regal figure, indeed a remarkable figure, was rising. She wore a crown at least as elaborate as the late Tsarina's of Russia (in fact it was that of 'Miss MEGATEST 1986–87') and her jewels were certainly as ornate. If there were any economies they were in her dress, which was scarcely anything more than an ermine bikini.

Even so, few Tsarinas could have commanded such a mighty roar as this pouting empress. James's binoculars slid from the brazen proportions of the suggestively waving woman to the far corner of the box. If he had had a glimpse of shameless glamour, he now had a close up view of its opposite. A sallow face twisted by malevolence, even though it purported to be smiling. A toad of a man half sunken in a wing collar and a velvet smoking jacket, encircled by equally ugly, if larger, men dressed in a similar style.

At last James knew where he was, just as, without introduction, he recognised the face he was looking at. A face well capable of stealing a child or an Ashes Urn! It could only belong to Ernie Tyburn himself, and this parody of a cricket match could only be another of his tasteless extravaganzas masquerading under the fair name of cricket.

Now James knew that the taxi driver had not delivered him to the hallowed portals of the Sydney Cricket Ground. He had dropped him at the gates of a kind of hell.

3

This day was also Sebastian Gover's first exposure to Megatest cricket. He had travelled by Australian Greyhound bus north from Adelaide as soon as it had become apparent to him that Scyld Berry would be continuing in his post as senior cricket correspondent of the *Observer* and that there were likely to be no further – certainly no immediate – calls on his pen. It was ever thus, Sebastian had thought, as he had thundered through the night in the company of loud-mouthed men detonating beer cans and prim women dressed like pages torn from 1950s editions of *Harpers Bazaar*. He had thought of the humiliations piled on the young Neville Cardus by the then *Manchester Guardian*, of Arlott forced to tramp an ordinary police constable's beat long after his early talent should have been recognised. And he had thought of Sub-Lieutenant Alan Ross RNVR, brutally pressganged for the wartime Russian convoys when any official with half an eye for language should have seen that his place was behind a microphone in Broadcasting House hymning the beauty of cricket to the occupied nations.

And he had reminded himself that like Ross's

74

Russian convoys and Arlott's pedestrian beat, this bus ride was but a prelude to inevitable discovery.

Meanwhile there remained the problem of earning a living beyond the five pounds per line his south-east England newspaper clients were prepared to pay, but then Sebastian Gover had reminded himself that he possessed in addition to a magic pen a sharp nose for a scoop. It had been alleged against him that he, alone among the correspondents of the London Sundays, had failed to lead with, or even note, the shock news of Brian Philpott's defection from the England camp to the Ernie Tyburn caravan.

Very well, he would be the first respectable writer to report on the Megatest Phenomenon. At the same time he would scoop the first appearance of England's renegade bowling hope in Megaworld colours. The *Observer* would have to think again.

'The Bacchic celebrations are over, not before time' his typewriter hammered in the speedily constructed luxury of the press box of Sydney's new Megatest Bowl.

Philpott returns to his mark looking a little ruefully at the skies. A mat of perspiration-sleeked hair is a mask to his inner thoughts. Does he wish these stark blue skies were a softer coloured English heaven? Is he thinking, perhaps with a shiver of nostalgia, of those gentle cumulus clouds, plump as baroque angels, which always seem to hover over the Stanley Barnes Stand at his native Edgbaston?

Certainly there is nothing of the dreamer about his run up. Some fast bowlers are two-year-olds, frisky and elegant as at the finishing post at Ascot. Others have the aggressive nimbleness of javelin throwers speeding soft-footed towards an appointment with the Persian hordes. Others are yeomen (such were Trueman and Statham our elders tell us). They move with bent back and grinding sinews towards the popping crease, as if labouring under the heavy pack it has always been a yeoman's lot to carry into England's wars. This then is Philpott bowling to Bloemfontein of Natal, whose colours are as vivid as the Orange Free State. A muscular deflection seeks to open his account (literally in Megatest terms); but a swoop and a throw, accurate as Robin Hood (in the guise of whom fine leg appears to be dressed), pins the Rebel South African to the crease.

This time Philpott's flaming missile is well pitched up outside the off stump. Bloemfontein essays a misguided cut and is rapped resoundingly in his Day-glo pads.

A raucous appeal climbs to the heavens. An oratorio chorus in which all the field joins with Philpott's base providing an orotund solo.

Umpire Wallace, imposing as a Pearly King (which indeed is how he is garbed), gravely considers the matter. Then seemingly unable to satisfy himself that the ball would have carried to second slip, takes the unprecedented step of consulting his colleague at square leg. From which position Bloemfontein is (though we must always defer in these matters to the Umpire's view and knowledge of the game) rather surprisingly given out.

Now we are treated to another officially-sponsored pitch invasion. 'The Field is full of *maids*,' to paraphrase Francis Thompson, though it is doubtful if this moral Victorian poet would have wholeheartedly approved of the jubilant ceremony that develops at the bowler's end.

The unfortunate Bloemfontein is the object of attention of another kind. The dear creatures of our childhood now appear in the role of tormentors. At the command of the duck, Donald, a gaggle of smiling cheerladies, roseate as Renoir nudes and nearly as undressed, empty a bucket of white feathers on the South African's head, while others treat him to a glutinous substance calculated to ensure the feathers' adhesion to his luckless person. It is, we are confidently assured by an invisible announcer, the traditional sentence on a player who twice fails to score in consecutive Megatests that he should be tarred in duck feathers. . . .

'Aggghh!' the writer Sebastian Gover suddenly screamed as he brought his fist down sharply on his typewriter keys. No other journalist turned from the field of play. Their binoculars stayed glued to the near-naked Renoir maids as Sebastian half sobbed, 'How can a serious writer describe a game like this? There can be no words, no felicitous metaphors for a Megatest. It is literally *indescribable!*'

4

It was time for the luncheon interval or, as the public address system preferred to describe it, 'Charlene's Lucky Mega Ticket Draw'. James Ball moved unsteadily towards the exit. Under the debris of his emotions was an instinct crying that it was going to take a very large gin and tonic in some cool and quiet place before any kind of recovery could be expected.

In this condition it was, perhaps, not so surprising that he failed for once to notice he was being followed. In a normal state of mind, he would probably have been alerted by the swarthy giant who had been lounging on the stand steps seemingly buried in an Arabic newspaper, a blackened cigarette end on his lower lip. As it was, he had passed with vacant eyes as the large, unkempt man folded his newspaper and followed him with a heavy soft-shoe shuffle. In fact James only became aware of him at the exit gate when he felt a hand on his shoulder, felt himself swung round like a turnstile and found himself staring up at a pustule-marked, moustachioed face breathing the abrasive scents of the bazaar's less popular juices.

'You have hashish, Mister?' the man demanded.

'Certainly not,' James answered, managing to convey a note of stern disapproval, despite the fact that both the giant's hands were now tightening on his neck.

'Hashish! Hashish! You have!'

'I don't smoke,' James gasped. 'Least of all your brand of poison!'

'Not you smoke, where is?' the giant roared, shaking the veteran spycatcher like a rabbit. 'You know where hashish is, you know who has the *hashish!*'

A memory of wartime training in Norwood floated into James's mind. He could almost smell the damp rising from the Nissen hut's concrete floor, a fairer smell by far than the scents that were now blasting into his face. The instructor's name was, if he remembered correctly, Major 'Batty' Bateman, a veteran of the Great War and probably of the Black and Tans. He could remember, almost word for word, the lecture this wiry, sinewy figure in singlet and shorts had delivered on the art of self defence, hands on hips in that fog-shrouded Nissen in the mists of past time.

'Now the conventional wisdom when you've got an ugly customer on your neck says "kick him in the balls!" I don't necessarily go along with this, not because it isn't cricket – we don't play cricket in this business – but because it doesn't always do the trick, particularly if you're an average sized bloke and you've got a great big hairy Hun on you. Landing a good kick in the balls is like place kicking in rugby: you've got to kick hard, you've got to kick up and if you're not careful you can misjudge the distance. That's why I say stamp like buggery on the bastard's toes. Whatever his size or yours you can't miss, and you've got Mother Gravity on your side. Come here Captain Ball and let me show what I mean. . . .'

Someone shivering in the back of the class had dared to object that the hairy Hun might be wearing the reinforced toe-cap of the standard German SS boot. James could not remember the discussion that followed, but in any case the problem did not arise here. His assailant was wearing a grease-marked pair of light shoes which might once have been described as 'brothel creepers'. James stamped down viciously, letting Mother Gravity guide him onto target. A gratifying if pungent howl went up from his attacker. This time James vaulted the turnstile as cleanly as Denis Compton.

Old Major 'Batty' Bateman had offered few words of counsel on what to do if the 'ugly customer' decided to give chase. But then the good Major could hardly have conceived of a customer with the strength to tear a turnstile apart with his bare hands before setting out in fiercely breathing pursuit.

Cars flashing past with horns blaring. Cars screeching, cars braking, drivers shouting obscene insults. But they are all foreign cars – American, Japanese, Italian, if not actually Australian, and their drivers swear in an almost foreign tongue. But suddenly – is he dreaming? – a Daimler door flies open and an English voice cries, 'For heaven's sake get in!'

5

'Are you sure you're all right?' Sandy Winchester was leaning from the front seat, a strained smile on his face.

'Perfectly thank you, Sandy. Though I will admit it's nice to be picked up by a Daimler. I didn't think you ran to them any more.'

Winchester flushed. 'This one's really for my own use. You'll have noticed I've taken the High Commission plates off it.'

'It was an agreeable coincidence running into you like this, anyway,' James panted as the hashish fiend took a final fist fling at the boot.

'Yes, wasn't it?' The seasoned diplomat turned a deeper shade of red, then asked with an air of uneasy nonchalance, 'Look James, I hope you weren't in anything like trouble back there, I mean serious trouble to do with the job everyone at the High Commission is hoping you really have left at home?'

James read the anxiety in his one-time associate's eyes, detected the undertone of fear in his bland words. The message was perfectly clear: the High Commission wanted a quiet life.

'Just a rather unsavoury drug pedlar,' James reassured. 'I should think one runs across quite a few of them in Sydney.'

'Hashish' the giant had seemed to be demanding. But why, James pondered, of him with such vicious insistence? James had a reasonable ear for Cairo dialects. As he replayed the threatening dialogue in his mind he came to the inexorable conclusion that he had misheard the unfriendly giant. It was not hashish but *the ashes* the villain was demanding. Why? It was a disturbing thought, not to be voiced to Sandy Winchester, particularly since under the elaborate disguise James was now certain he had recognised his old antagonist of Suez Crisis days – Colonel Nepfar Alim of the Egyptian Security Services.

Pre-Test Trials

1

'Good luck, Curly my old mate!' Wally Ficket bellowed, raising a pint to the incoming batsman, David Gower. 'And remember what I was telling you over the bevies last night. We all go through these bad patches; believe me, my son, I've been there myself. Just play your natural game, Goldie my old chum, and let the Aussies worry about the runs!'

If their guide had succeeded in establishing any social contact with the ex England Captain so far this tour, James Ball was unaware of it. The impromptu visit to the Sydney Hilton had failed to yield a single member of the England touring party who, it had later been discovered, were staying at the Hyde Park Plaza. A raid on this hotel the following evening had succeeded in trapping the reserve wicketkeeper writing postcards home in the television lounge, but had produced no other scalps. Ficket's suggestion, on the following day, that they should attempt to ambush the England party after nets at the Sydney Cricket Ground had been vetoed by the Kangaroo tourists in favour of watching a repeat of an Australian TV's 'Bodyline' epic in the comfort of The Ned Kelly. 'At least we can be sure of seeing Douglas Jardine,' a Derbyshire member had caustically cracked.

But what did all this really matter? James Ball

was watching cricket, not some garish travesty. There could be no doubt that this was the authentic, immense Sydney Cricket Ground and the sparsely peopled promontory over there was the legendary Hill, and that what they were witnessing was the traditional Pre-Test fixture of the MCC v an Australian XI, and that the sun was shining on white flannels. Handsome enough compensation for the fact that the MCC had lost an early wicket and Wally was making another exhibition of himself.

'See the new ball off, David, and you've got a pint on me tonight, old son – and that's a promise. You just give 'em hell from your old Uncle Wally!'

The ex-Derbyshire man turned, a sunlit beer in hand, from the field of play with a smile that seemed to invite the approval of his party. In the case of Percy Gwynne-Watson this was not forthcoming. The sight of white flannels on green sward had acted on him like an anaesthetic. He was sleeping in a dream-world of political violence while his wizened wife watched with glazed eyes that saw nothing, least of all the point of a married life, half of which seemed to have been spent at Test matches in the company of a comatose husband. Next to this couple sat another who only had eyes for each other. This was the doting pair who had left Heathrow wearing matching Free Forest blazers. Now they were locked together under what at first glance suggested one outsize I Zingari garment but which on closer inspection could be seen to be two. As Jan had sharply riposted more than once on the trip, 'Does it matter what they're entitled to wear? Their sex lives have certainly worn better than ours, darling!'

None of the party, least of all Wally Ficket, had noticed that James and Jan, sitting further back in the stand, had landed the first real catch of the tour. At this moment James was in discreet conversation with his old friend Miles Pershore, Manager of England in Australia.

'Thankfully this is not the West Indies, but I can't pretend we don't have our worries,' the former Leicestershire amateur captain and Treasury mandarin confided. 'We're not too worried about that upset in Western Australia – we had the best of the draw at Adelaide; but we are a little worried about David's form – oh dear he's out again! – and we are a little nervous about more desertions to Tyburn, though here we do have an excellent local lawyer. Don't quote me, but we're also rather concerned about the tour itinerary, particularly this fixture to Jum Jum which they've inserted at the last minute on the eve of the second Test at Perth.'

'Where is Jum Jum?' Jan wondered.

'Exactly. We are all stumped by that one. Apparently it's a small island off Arnhem Land in the Northern Territory. You can't actually see it on the map, but I'm reliably informed it's somewhere in the Arafura Sea.'

The Arafura Sea was not a stretch of water which was often in James Ball's thoughts, but it had floated into them comparatively recently. Why? And in what connection? It irritated James, once renowned for an ICL computer-like memory, when things got lost in his mind's venerable data bank; so it was a relief to be able to locate the answer comparatively speedily. A recent *Times* obituary. The death of Sir Gervase Spooner. Fellow he had met at Swindon in the war who had left the Service under something of a cloud. His later years spent on the Coburn Peninsula 'in the Arafura Sea'.

'That's quite a long way north,' James smiled with modest pride in his memory.

'It's a hell of a long way north,' Pershore warmly concurred. 'Especially when you bear in mind that our chaps will have just come through the Brisbane Test, which is always a stinker, and needing to get into shape for the Test at Perth which is traditionally a happy hunting ground for Australian fast bowlers. Strictly between ourselves we've made the strongest representation to the Australian authorities – pointed out as politely as possible that this Jum Jum junket is going to knock the stuffing completely out of our chaps at a vital stage of the series; but they're absolutely adamant. Apparently there's this Mr Money Bags, name of Tyrone Marshall, who's got a big off-shore operation up there and wants cricket to show the flag in what is quite clearly a barbaric region; but more to the point he's prepared to put enough cash into conventional Aussie cricket to enable them to buy some of their chaps back from Tyburn. But that's not going to do our cause any good if we come to the Third Test two down in the series.'

'Have you asked the High Commission in Canberra to use their good offices?' James enquired.

'Exactly what the TCCB suggested; but I'm afraid they've been rather less than helpful – oh dear, Gatting's gone! – a lot of talk about our role as ambassadors for a "caring Commonwealth" (not that anyone's going to care too much in Jum Jum; we gather it's got a native population of approximately twenty drop-outs, half of them aborigines, and endless bromides on the necessity of not stepping on the Aussies' *amour propre*, which they insist on reminding us is in a pretty sensitive state after all the Tests they've lost. Damn it, we could do with a win as much as anyone! Personally I came away with the impression that Her Majesty's High Commission wouldn't at all mind if we lost the Ashes. And that's another thing, isn't it? Even if we keep them, we seem to have lost the Urn. Don't repeat this, but the team has opened a book on the likeliest culprit and I can tell you, the big money is on Ernie Tyburn. Still I daresay you've got your own view on that, James. Between ourselves, how close are you chaps on Tyburn's noxious scent, and what are the chances of getting him to disgorge?'

'I will repeat the statement I made at Colombo, Miles,' James said with just a hint of severity in his tone. 'I am *retired* from the Service and I am here on *holiday* to watch . . .' Then it hit him.

2

'Gatting takes guard like a Grenadier,' Sebastian Gover had been pounding at the back of the press box.

It could be the Somme or it could be Waterloo, England's Waterloo! Gower is out, and the age of chivalry is dead. Now only solid professionalism can hope to plug the gap torn in England's ranks. The exigencies of test warfare have created him Captain, yet the man who surveys Border's field placings is essentially a non-commissioned officer, the product of years of hard drill under the Sergeant Majors of the MCC's own Purbright at the Nursery End at Lord's. 'Keep your bat straight and your chin up, Gatting!' deep monitory voices call to him across the years. And this is precisely what this war-scarred old trooper does as he prepares to face the Gower-slayer, Merv Hughes.

The crack of a rifle shot, and Gatting and Broad cross twice which by any mathematical equation makes two. Hughes drops his next missile shorter. Gatting flashes a stroke which would have earned him a savage reprimand back at his St John's Wood barracks; but here on a tropical day at Sydney it gets him a four, which is as unsoldierly as a Central American irregular. 'Remember the Sergeant Majors of St John's Wood, Guardsman Gatting,' every Englishman on the ground silently implores. Our prayers are not answered. Wicketkeeper, slips and bowler are convulsed in a triumphant war dance, albeit, mercifully, without the blatant indecorum which is a feature of so-called 'Megatests'!

'*Le Garde recule!*' as Napoleon cried on a fateful Belgian hillside, and we share something of his agony as we watch Guardsman Gatting walking slowing back to the pavilion. Is it our bruised imagination which seems to see a boomerang twirl triumphantly over the field of play – a field which belongs to an Australian XI, at least as your correspondent writes – and then arcs impudently back to the stand from whence it came?

3

In fact the boomerang was not a figment of Sebastian Gover's imagination. It had discharged from somewhere behind the row where the Balls were sitting with the Manager of MCC in Australia and on its whirling return it felled James with a vicious slash to the temple.

'Oh matey, what have you done? You didn't listen to your Uncle Wally did you!' Ficket cried, but he was addressing the departing figure of Mike Gatting, not the crumpled body of James Ball.

'What is your purpose in visiting Australia?' the immigration officer enquired.

The visitor tapped his dark glasses reflectively. Then he answered firmly, 'Cricket. I am here to observe the cricket.'

The immigration officer glanced again at the man's Yugoslav passport, comparing the photographed face with dark glasses with the face that hovered over his desk. 'What brings you all the way from Zagreb to see a team like our mob?' he asked.

'Yes I am following the Ash, ASHOO,' the visitor answered with an explosive sneeze.

'Caught a bit of a cold have you?' the officer queried.

'It is nothing,' the visitor gestured although, in fact, the cold he was suffering from had nearly been the death of him. I. Smirnov had hardly touched down at Tashkent, back in Soviet territory, before he was whisked northwards by an Air Force plane to a Moscow gripped by an early winter. They had kept him waiting for two hours in the icy corridors of the Marshal Vorishilov Buildings, yet this had been warmer than the interview that followed.

'Can you provide us with any convincing reason, Comrade,' they had asked when the chilling recriminations over the failed hijack had finally ceased, 'why you should not be treated for serious mental disorder at a correction camp at Nordvik in the Arctic Sea?'

He was being roughly manhandled towards the door when the answer had suddenly come to him, 'Because I am the only man in the service who understands how to follow the cricket!' he had yelled.

'That is incorrect,' his interrogators had finally

answered after a long whispered consultation. 'Agent Stephanie is thoroughly familiar with the cricketering and she is already operating in Australia.'

'Agent Stephanie is not even knowing who is W. G. Grass!' Smirnov had cried in the doorway, desperate to buy time.

'She is proficient enough to have led the Hague Women's Elevenses to the conquest of all Holland,' his interrogators had sternly replied after another whispered consultation, 'and simultaneously to have neutralised effectively the principal Netherlands missile bases.'

'Mike Gatty, Davies Gowe, Robert Wills, Jam Brearley, Ian Botham, Jam Brearley, Tony Grog, Mick Dennis, Rillingworth . . . see, I can remember back all the English captains to the anti-Fascist War!' screamed I. Smirnov, finding that under pressure he had recalled almost completely a whole page of the brief that had been issued to him before his last mission to England. 'Can Agent Stephanie retain data like these?'

He was out in the icy corridor, except for his two hands which were still gripping the door frame in spite of the battering they were receiving from the KGB heavyweight who was opening and closing the door on them, when his chief interrogator, or at least the grey face seated at the centre of the three-man tribunal, announced, 'I have please one more question to put to the comrade.'

The question was simply this: 'Comrade I. Smirnov, will you please tell the enquiry what are the origins of the talismanic "Ashes" which are superstitiously worshipped at the Museum of the Lord's at St John's Wood, London?'

'They are being the gift of Miss Florrie Morphy of

Sunbury, Victoria, to her English lover the sadistic naval officer Captain Bligh, later Earl of the Darnley,' Smirnov answered he knew not how. The veteran KGB agent did not believe in miracles, therefore he could only suppose he must have memorised that eighty-six page brief on the organisation of English cricket in its entirety. In any case, he found that the heavyweights were suddenly dusting his suit instead of trying to tear it to shreds, and later in another corridor he was being issued with a false passport by a near smiling female official.

True, they had taken their revenge in a small way. The purpose of the mission to Australia had not been made entirely clear to him, and it had been stressed that he was to take his orders from the detested Agent Stephanie. In addition, they had kept him waiting for two hours on a disused runway of Moscow's arctic airport for his flight to Zagreb.

'Are you sure you haven't caught anything infectious?' the immigration officer wanted to know.

'It is nothing but a sneeze in a handkerchief,' I Smirnov casually answered.

'We don't welcome migrants to Australia,' the official cautioned him, 'particularly migrants with infectious diseases. I'm giving you a three-week visitor's permit, strictly to watch the cricket. Stay a day longer, and I'll get the bloody Wallabies to take you apart.'

'Thank you so kindly,' said I. Smirnov. He could tell by the underarm sweat patches on the official's shirt that he had arrived in a kinder, warmer climate.

Intensive Cares

Sometimes he dreamed he was playing the bowling of Malcolm Marshall without a helmet, and that no matter how he ducked and weaved that lethally fast short-pitcher kept finding his savaged temple. At other times he seemd to be in a KGB or Gestapo cell. They had found a way they believed might make him talk – and this was the continuous application of a surgical hammer to the boomerang wound. In other slightly less painful moments of delirium he heard the booming voice of Sir Hector Bootle repeatedly demanding to know the score from Jum Jum.

Only very slowly (he could not measure the days) did James Ball become aware that the white ceiling on which his painful fantasies danced belonged to a private hospital. It was later still before he was able to track the sweet smell that had attended all his alarming dreams to the sheafs of sub-tropical flowers parked on a flickering but silent colour television set, and in a jab of memory he was grateful to Jan for insisting that they take out medical insurance at Heathrow Airport.

He was vaguely conscious of visitors. Buxom, tanned and friendly Australian nurses with ice buckets, pleasantly and maternally scolding, as if he were a little boy who had got himself into an imprudent scrap.

A face he was almost certain belonged to Miles

Pershore, Manager of England in Australia repeating 'You never know these days, but that thing could have been meant for me.'

Certainly he was visited by the anxiously smiling face of Sandy Winchester of the High Commission in Canberra. 'We're all praying it was an accident,' James thought he heard him say. 'The last thing we want at this moment is any evidence that you're a target of hostility down here.'

And of course there was Jan, glittering and glamorous in the jewellery of their courtship and the summer fashions of Harvey Nichols. He had not seen her looking so desirable for many years. He had the uneasy sensation that she might have fallen in love again, an impression that was reinforced by the heavy scent of a Right Bank *parfumerie* – always a tell-tale sign of another adventure in what had been a rich, and for James often distressing, emotional life.

'You're managing to get along all right without me?' he asked one morning or afternoon. They were the first coherent words he had uttered since the accident.

'Look, I've brought you the papers from home,' she answered indirectly, planting a loving and odorous kiss on his bandaged forehead, and was gone.

It was good to feel the texture of *The Times* again, if it was not quite the graphic pleasure it had been before the transfer to Wapping. Even the coarser grained *Daily Express* produced comforting home thoughts from abroad.

The London papers were now mourning for two disasters – the theft of the Ashes Urn and the more recent defection of England's fast bowling hope, Brian Philpott, to the Tyburn camp. The two events were combined in an *Express* leader, supporting a front-page demand to **BRING THEM HOME!**, that saw the wily Tyburn behind both savage blows to the health of English cricket. Sandy Winchester will have a stroke when he reads this, James found he was alert enough to smile to himself.

Was it this day or the day after that the door of his private room flew open and a large nurse of swarthy complexion commanded: 'Now you strip!'?

'You don't sound Australian,' James observed as his bedclothes were ripped off.

'Yes I Aussie all right, I imigranti. Now you strip off!'

'A migrant? Where from?'

'You know Rumaanyer. That where my folk from. You strip quick please.'

'Rumania. I understand now. But why do I have to strip?'

'Massage. You are old man. You lie in bed too long. You get sores and orithritas. You need handling heavy.'

In accelerating panic, James sought to pull up his pyjama trousers, but realised he had none. He had been issued with the traditional hospital smock.

'You don't strip, I strip you,' the migrant nurse informed him as two large hands sundered even this fragile protection.

'Have you any news of the match against an Australian XI?' James enquired defensively. He felt a bulging stockinged knee pressing onto his never robust chest. 'But then I suppose you don't follow the cricket much.'

'Oh yes, like you much am following the cricket Mr Ball!' Immense white teeth, and lips fringed above by the ghost of a moustache, came into ferocious close-up. 'Like you, Mr Ball, I and my friends we very

92

interested in the Tests; we interested to do know why they lose those Hashes. But we are thinking you are knowing where those Hashes are being. Where those Hashes, Mr Ball?'

James started to scream in pain as he was savagely wrenched in an area where he was later to decide that if he was ever to be admitted to an Australian hospital again he would wear a protective box. His mouth was immediately closed by a hand as capacious as Rodney Marsh's.

'Listen now, Mr Ball, I give you a choice,' the ministering migrant hissed. 'I can be hard with you, or I can be good to you, even thought you are an old man I will try very heavily to give you pleasure. But you must in any case swear to me who is stealing the Hashes otherwise I will be very hurtful to you.' As if to emphasise the point, the massively built masseuse of Rumanian extraction brought her other knee, and therefore the weight of her whole body, to rest on his abdomen.

'Jan, thank God, you're here!' Only a splutter escaped the suffocating hand on his mouth. But surely he was not dreaming. Jan was framed in the doorway with a fresh batch of newspapers from home. But now what was hopefully not a dream became a development in an increasingly horrifying nightmare. Jan, with only the minutest lift of an eyebrow, was discreetly closing the door again. He heard her high heels clicking away down the corridor like a vanishing hope.

Nothing left but to race the mind back to that damp Nissan hut in Norwood and try and remember if Major 'Batty' Bateman had had any words of advice on what you did when you had a heavy-weight nurse of Rumanian extraction squeezing the life out of you

93

in a number of excruciating ways. As it happened some fragments of counsel drifted back to him over the years:

'Never trust a woman . . . specially the Hibernian variety. In Cork . . . this so called tea-lady . . . a rabid Fenian underneath . . . came at me when I was kipping without my Sam Browne . . . fingers in the eyes, knee in the groin, the usual stuff . . . only one answer, bite her nose like your life depends on it, and cling on like a terrier!'

The nurse had a large peasant nose, and it was within range. James bit it as if his life depended on it. A scream like the Balkans rent by yet another atrocious war. Then a savage jerking back of the head which lifted James bodily out of his hospital bed. Now with hot, breathy demented yells the giantess tried to shake herself free of him. James was surprised at her failure. At an optimistic estimate two thirds of his jaw had, over the years, become dependent on bridgework and various dentures. At each violent shaking of the mighty Slav's head he expected to hear the disintegration of all this painstaking dentistry. But he clung on like a terrier, as Major Bateman had advised, and in the end it was the would-be masseuse who slumped to the floor and James who rang the bell for assistance.

'What were you thinking of, leaving me with that creature?' James asked his wife when later that day (he knew it was the same day because he discharged himself immediately after the incident) they were returning by taxi to The Ned Kelly.

'Darling, you've always been so tolerant of my little skirmishes.'

'That's not an answer.'

Jan pretended to be exploring the altitude of the

Centre Point tower. 'I thought you wanted to be left alone with that little nurse,' she finally admitted. 'I thought I owed you an innocent fling or two.'

'Little nurse? Did you see the size of that monster? How can you possibly have imagined . . . ?'

Jan turned from the tower to give her husband's head bandages an affectionate pat. 'Darling, please don't get overwrought. The Head Nurse particularly said it's bad for you to get worked up.'

'Nurses! I never want to see a nurse in my life again!' James shuddered.

The telephone rang seconds after they had got back to their hotel bedroom.

'At last you're answering,' a distant yet powerful voice reproached. 'I've been ringing all over Australia for you. Why? To tell you your flat's been broken into – that's why!' Sir Hector Bootle boomed across the continents and oceans.

'Has anything valuable been taken?' James moaned, thinking of his 1900–1985 collection of *Wisden*, his signed copy of K. S. Ranjitsinhji's *Jubilee Book of Cricket* and his first editions of *Felix on the Bat* and Pyecroft's *The Cricket Field*.

'Just private papers. I daresay they'll be returned to you in due course.'

'You mean you have arrested the perpetrators?'

'You're not listening to what I'm saying,' he was answered by a Baskerville bark that defied geography. 'Your flat has been broken into by Harry Grimaldi and the Pitch Rollers on my orders. Don't sound so civic-righteously shocked, James. You've been so damned dilatory about this Ashes business we were bound to wonder if you've been squared by the other side. So far as we have been able to ascertain – by the way, isn't it time you paid your subscription to the Civil Service Motoring Club? – you're in the clear on that one. But that doesn't remove the fact that you've got absolutely nowhere in your efforts, if you've made any, to retrieve the Urn.'

'Hector, I think there may be rather more to this than we at first supposed.'

'Speak up, I can't hear you. You're not round the corner, you know. No, you can leave the Dresden china, Harry!'

'Where are you calling from, Hector?' James enquired with a shudder of apprehension.

'From your flat, where do you think? You don't expect me to go out to a phone box in this weather, do you?'

'Hector, please hang up,' James implored. 'Do you realise how much it costs to ring Australia these days?'

'I certainly shall not hang up. Not after calling every hotel in Sydney to find where the hell you are. I've never talked to so many cretinous and imbecilic hotel clerks in all my life!'

'Hector, if you don't hang up, I will. I simply cannot afford this kind of extravagance in my circumstances.'

'If you try and hang up, James, I will have no hesitation in calling you back immediately. I won't hang up until I have a detailed report on your enquiries so far – on the charitable assumption that you've made any. It's all very well for you to sit around on some beach while Jan makes cow's eyes at the surf riders; but I've got the police on my back, who've got the media and the MCC on their backs, saying you and I promised to crack this one pronto.'

'Hector, wouldn't it really be more sensible to ring me in the morning – from *your office?*'

'You don't catch me that easily, you crafty old sluggard. Don't think I don't know your time is upside down down there. If I rang in the morning, you'd be asleep. But then you're usually asleep in the daytime as well, aren't you, James? In fact, if you don't mind me being utterly frank, I'm beginning to have serious doubts about the wisdom of entrusting you with this mission. You seem to have drawn a complete blank, notwithstanding the fact we gave you a bloody good steer, practically talked you onto your target. I refer, of course, to Mr "Bernie Thighburn", rhymes with you-know-who I trust!'

'Hector, there are certain developments in this case I think you should know . . .' James began, then abruptly stopped himself. He thought of the time it would take to explain his suspicions about the so-called masseuse of Rumanian extraction, the apparent accident of the boomerang and the extraordinary encounter with his old antagonist Colonel Alim of the Egyptian Security Services. And of the extra time it would take to expound his theories on the motive behind the near-fatal collision with the mystery beer crates, and his sixth sense that the hijacking over the Bay of Bengal may not have been entirely uncon-nected with his visit to Australia. Even that the self-professed cricket enthusiast, Steve Burbek from Newark, New Jersey, may not have been all he seemed.

Given time he would like to have discussed with his controller the seemingly incredible possiblity that for some unfathomable reason the whole espionage world had an interest in the theft of the Ashes Urn; but his brave heart recoiled from the further digits all this would add to his violated telephone bill. 'Message received and out,' he said.

'No it's damned well not out,' Sir Hector Bootle blazed back. 'You've left me no alternative but to do all your homework for you. I've had to pull every string in the book, ring around everyone we know in Sydney and Canberra, to get you into cahoots with friend Bernie Fryburn – rhymes with Tyburn for Christ's sake!'

'I hope not at my expense, Hector,' James involuntarily interjected.

'The big expense has been on my very valuable time,' Sir Hector Bootle huffed. 'You ought to be bloody grateful to me for wangling you an invitation to the grisly little convict's next thrash – do I have to do all your work for you? Anyway, James, I can assure you that as far as he's concerned you're an absolute nobody!'

'Receptionist, we are receiving no more calls under any circumstances,' were Ball's last words before he fell into a deep, protective sleep.

Doubting Castle

Sir Hector Bootle had been as good as his word. The next morning's post had contained a panoramic gold embossed card which had read:

Mr Ernest Greg Tyburn, OBE
has the honour to request the pleasure of your Company
at an informal reception to mark the acquisition
of the
SRI LANKAN TEST SQUAD
for
MEGATEST CRICKET

Dress Formal

'He spells company with a capital C' remarked James as their taxi cruised along the fringe of a pink Pacific dotted with sails spread out like fielders towards Ernest Tyburn's retreat in the desirable Kilogola Plateau suburb.

'I suppose because he's rather a commercial little man,' answered Jan, who was, incidentally, dressed to kill and looking at least a half million Australian dollars. 'He probably thinks people are companies rather than individuals.'

'Or perhaps he's merely uneducated.'

'Darling, you are a snob!'

'Yet despite his formal education, Master Tyburn will doubtless prove an engaging host. It could be a delightful party. One never knows.'

'One never knows. That's always the fun of parties, isn't it?' Jan blushed becomingly in the mother of pearl evening.

'Star'd at the Pacific . . . with a wild surmise,' said James.

'What are you talking about now?'

'Stout Cortez and all his men "Silent, upon a peak in Darien" – Keats, of course,' Ball dreamily replied. 'All this silent sea reminded me of it – I mean the "wild surmise". What do we surmise? Certainly that we have embarked, like stout Cortez indeed, on a journey with more ramifications than we had at first anticipated. We thought we were merely following a cricket tour, but already we have encountered strangers who are manifestly not playing cricket and now we are headed, not by our own volition, to what appears to be a cricket occasion of sorts, but which could turn out to be a very different kind of encounter.'

'Darling, I wonder if it wouldn't have been best to leave you at the hotel. I'm not sure you should even be up yet.'

James impatiently brushed the suggestion aside. 'We go to beard the ogre in his domain,' he said. 'Will we get a glimpse of the chalice? And if so what are the perils in the way of retrieving it? Will we capture the golden fleece, or find we have merely turned another corner in a baffling maze? You see what I mean by "wild surmise"?'

Jan was gazing at her husband, rather than the Pacific, with a measure of surmise. 'Darling, are you going to keep that hat on all evening?' she enquired.

James was wearing a trilby (the Sandown model from Locke's) well down on his forehead to mask the still stitched antiseptic-tinted boomerang wound.

'Perhaps you would recommend a helmet,' he countered. 'I grant you it's prudent to be prepared for "bouncers" on this tour.'

It was dusk as they drove on from the maximum security gates up the long soundless tarmacadam driveway to the Tyburn mansion. There was still light enough to see the turquoise folds of Ku-Ring-Gai Chase National Park on the opposite shore of Pittwater Bay, but already Tyburn's lawns and groves were sewn with luminous Chinese lanterns. And now it could be seen that the vast mansion itself – an architectural anthology of Spanish, Georgian and Italian styles – was bathed in floodlights, although this may have been for security reasons.

A mixed reception committee was greeting guests in the massive doorway. A butler tried to take James's hat while a Tyburn heavy rigorously frisked him. These formalities over, a carnation was lingeringly pressed into his buttonhole by a provocatively pouting Megatest scantily-clad. Meanwhile another near topless hostess presented Jan with a complimentary carrier bag of cosmetics with the Tyburn Leisure Industries label.

Now the couple advanced tentatively into the interior. James was reminded of a West End musical he had seen on leave towards the end of the War. What was its name? No matter. The twin staircase, draped with champagne swillers, had put him in mind of the show's lavish final number about how it would be when the lights came on in London once again. But they hadn't been able to run to fountains in this wartime extravaganza and the chorus girls, eager to please as they may have been, had remained well within the bounds of decorum, which could not be

101

said of the dishevelled Australian nymphs who were lurching across his field of vision.

'I should be very surprised if we know anyone here,' James said *sotto voce*.

But Jan was already waving to a familiar face. As it loomed closer, James also recognised the features of a man who had once captured five English wickets before lunch at 'headquarters'. He had last seen this face perspiring proudly as he led the Pakistan team up the pavilion steps. It was perspiring even more profusely now.

'My so darling Mrs Ball, it such a poem to see you!' cried the great Pakistan and Hampshire all-rounder, Mohamad Sindh. 'You know you are like a puff of fresh air.' He waved the hand that had once slipped a fast inswinger under Geoffrey Boycott's defensive forward stroke, hustled David Gower into a shameful played on and conned Chris Tavare into an uncharacteristic and fatal slash, this and more one June morning at Lord's. 'You are a wonderful lady, very kind and infinite in wisdom. No one is as sympathetic as you in these Megatests!' The dinner-jacketed legend kissed Jan's cheek. 'Yes, young girls without their clothes. Yes, always the promise of the exquisite Charlene. But you know, Mrs Ball, always the hearts are like cold iron. They say I am owing them two hundred thousand dollars Australian and must be tarfeathered with the duck. *You* never ask me to bat in turban and ceremonial robes of an Afghan Freedom Fighter. Oh Mrs Ball, I miss balls without you!' He was clearly drunk.

'I promise never to do anything in public to shame you,' Jan had once undertaken in fraught confrontation half a lifetime and half a world away one early morning in St John's Wood. It looked now as if, even though unwittingly, that this promise was about to be broken, as the distraught Asian athlete plunged a hand into the frothy folds of Jan's Harvey Nichols ball gown.

It far from suits my purpose, but I will have to remonstrate with him, James was just starting to think to himself when the ex-Pakistan and Hampshire all-rounder and recent Megatest acquisition slumped to the floor.

'And once was I being the horror of the English dressing rooms,' he moaned. 'Oh Allah forgive me, I wish on this Tyburn only the death of suffocation by dried camel dung!'

'He could have overtaken Ian Botham for wickets and run aggregates in Tests,' James remarked stonily as he tugged his wife clear of the ruin of Pakistan's international aspirations. 'I didn't know you had met him before.'

Jan too deliberately shrugged. 'Just a cup of tea in the Members and Friends Stand. They don't usually drink, you know.'

James wished he could have taken her at her word; but his near infallible memory back-tracked to the sequel of that dramatic morning at Lord's, which had seen England reeling at the luncheon interval. One of the resumption of play, there was a public announcement which, at the time, had come as a balm to James – as it must have done to every other patriot on the ground: 'Abdul Kasingh is fielding as substitute for Mohamad Sindh, who is indisposed.' But now he wondered, or rather suspected. After all, there had been similar unaccountable 'indispositions' on the part of tourists dating as far back as the New Zealand series in 1937 which, as it happened, had been Jan's first introduction to Test matches.

'Can we return to the business at hand?' he suggested without overmuch conjugal affection. But now Jan was waving at another familiar face, as a canary coloured dinner jacket reeled from the crowded staircase. 'Jan, fabulous Earth Mother, thank God you're here!'

'Bill!' cried Jan.

Bill, thought James, Bill Regan, former Australian Test skipper and widely trumpeted Megatest acquisition. He had wept publicly to the media on the occasion of his replacement as captain and he was weeping unashamedly now. James thought nostalgically of his grim forerunners – Warwick Armstrong, 'Horseshoe' Collins, Bradman, Laurie and Simpson. He was doubtful if anyone of them had ever had occasion to show the press so much as a moistened eye.

'The man is a monster, a beast!' the ex-skipper literally cried. 'Would you believe he's had the nerve to drop me for Brisbane, Australia v the Superpowers, despite the fact that I've scored $Aus2000,000 this season *and* won the golden basket for catches against the South African Rebels at Melbourne? I tell you, darling, it makes me absolutely sick. In fact I shouldn't be surprised if I *am* sick on this filthy champagne. Oh my kind, comforting, adorable Mother Goose, isn't there somewhere we can go and hold hands!'

James watched his wife being towed away into the mêlée of guests. He made no attempt to intervene. She could come to no real harm with Bill Regan!

'Mr James Ball of MI5, or is it MI6?' James stiffened and turned to face whoever it was who clearly knew too much.

He was looking at a crafty pair of eyes and an

almost toothless smile. Like himself, the man was wearing a hat, but his was a Pearly King's, as was his jacket which extended, like an umpire's coat, nearly to his knees.

'We've only met the once, Mr Ball, and that not under the most agreeable of circumstances. To tell you the honest truth there was a time when I and my good ladies had cause to revile the very mention of you. The name is Peat, Reg Peat, if by any chance that rings a bell.'

'The fourth Test at Trent Bridge!'

'A draw due to interruption of light and other acts of nature. I had to wrestle as never before with my professional integrity, but I delivered the result you wanted, Mr Ball,' confessed the former Test umpire. 'By so doing I enabled my country to square the series and retain the Ashes at the Oval. But at what cost to myself, Mr Ball, sir! I had, foolishly, no doubt, fancied that I might be the recipient of civic honours, or at least a couple of grand under the table. As you may recall, squire, my reward was a prison cell without so much as a black and white TV.'

An Australian summer of desperate war against I. Smirnov of the KGB and the far more sinister Agent Stephanie – James remembered it all too well, and the price that had to be paid in terms of conventional morality, as well as money. He felt an unpleasant flush on his cheek. 'I'm afraid we were playing for higher stakes than the Ashes,' he said. 'In any case if I remember correctly, a discreet pardon was arranged immediately the season was over.'

'Bless you, squire, I don't bear you any grudges now. In fact, you might say you did me a favour. You see there wasn't much work around when I got out of Strangeways. The season, as you say, was over, and no one was hurrying to talk about me standing again the next summer. Then I saw a newspaper piece about these Megatests. I said to myself and the good ladies, "Australia here we come!" I can tell you we've never looked back.'

'It would certainly appear to be a different kind of game.'

James started to edge away, but a sinewy hand restrained him by the sleeve. 'There's a lot more money in it, comrade. Well, you've only got to look at the scoreboard. These young Megastars aren't playing for peanuts, believe me. A good innings can make a man's fortune – a couple of upheld appeals, and he's back in Queer Street. There's a lot more incentive about the game, you might say. And then,' a bushy eyebrow descended in a conspiratorial wink, 'you'd be surprised how many of the young gentlemen fancy their chances as the escort at the leisure complex of their choice of that tasty bit of crumpet, Mademoiselle Charlene! So you see, an umpire carries a heavy burden of responsibility out there in the Megarena, Mr Ball. He cannot but be aware of the immense sums that hang upon his judgement – the aspirations for untold wealth and fabulous sexuality that depend on the merest movement of his forefinger. It gives a man a strange sense of power and also, you might say, an opportunity to recoup the lifestyle he's sacrificed in his country's service. You'd be amazed how rewarding it can prove to take your eye off the ball in this game. No need to look down your nose, squire, I can assure you I have retained my basic scruples. In my book a bloody Yorkshireman is still plum in front, even if he's wearing Megatest colours and he's slipped me the odd van-load of vodka to get unsighted by the glare. Do you use these?' The umpire casually proffered a box of Havanas.

'Peat, you are an incorrigible . . .' James was going to say 'rogue', and further add that he was a disgrace to the game of cricket. But then he reminded himself that Megatests were not cricket and besides, all conversation had now been hushed by an erupting internal communications system.

'My lords, ladies and gentlemen, please be silent for your host, the distinguished industrialist and cricket benefactor, Mr Ernest Greg Tyburn OBE!'

'Guests and friends of Megatest cricket,' a nasal, up-country accent crawled out of a dozen or more concealed speakers, 'I am sorry I am not able to address all of you personally. As you will appreciate there are a lot of you here tonight, and there just isn't room for you all even in my private suites. But I do have some very welcome guests here with me – and that's the entire Sri Lankan Test squad. And don't believe any media monkey who tells you I haven't scooped all their key players: I've got every man jack of them on my payroll!'

Applause, but not where James was standing at a decent remove from Umpire Peat. Not, indeed, from any of the champagne slurpers spread around this Astaire and Rogers film set of a hall. All the same, the applause was raucous. Possibly the guests privileged to be admitted to Tyburn's private suites had more to drink, or perhaps the clapping was manufactured.

'I want you to give a big welcome to these brave little players from Colombo . . .' More applause, real or pre-recorded. ' . . . give them a hearty welcome to *real* competitive cricket. I want them to know, and I want the media to take note, that they will be competing on equal terms with all my white players and rebel blacks. There is no colour bar in Megatest cricket. Every player, be he white, black or tea-stained, has an equal opportunity to win the same astronomical cash rewards and leisure prizes. I may add that I have it from the lady in person that no racial discrimination will be shown to the lucky winner of the super prize of escort to the tantalising sex-goddess Charlene at the Tyburn Leisure Complex of his choice. So let's say to our new Sri Lankan friends "start belting that leather, Jimbos!" '

2

'You are, if I may say please, looking a little lost.'

James had pushed his way through chambers of guests in search of air and had finally found it beside a lake of a swimming pool in which the more inebriated guests were splashing, some of them in the nude.

She was dressed, or rather undressed, in the 'uniform' of a Megatest hostess. A sparse costume of scarlet silk, cut as low as a bikini with a transparent letter M at the midriff; her legs being sheathed in gold cable tights.

It was an inappropriate costume for the cricket field at any time on anybody, in James's view, but it looked particularly unsuitable on an oriental. Eastern allure, to his mind, was not to be expressed in the crude trappings of the Playboy Club or the raucous beauty contest. In any case, the girl's endowments were not such as to produce vulgar whistles from half intoxicated businessmen. She had firm but slight breasts and there was nothing statuesque about her modest proportions. That she was an attractive little creature was not in doubt, but it was a body that demanded a kimono; in the garb of a Megatest hostess it was degraded. So it was with a touch of compassion as well as gratitude that he answered the girl.

'Thank you, my dear, I was merely looking for air; it is a little close inside.'

'No. You are looking for something more, I can tell,' the girl insisted. 'I am, what is the word you have – clairvoice.'

'You mean clairvoyant.'

'Yes, I can see so many things about people. Many things about you.'

'Such as, for instance? I can assure you I am a very dull cove.'

Now he allowed her to lead him to a seat out of the poolside's glare. It was dark, but he had the impression they were surrounded by extravagant vegetation. The air oozed the scents of nature at its most exotic, and somewhere in the background an orchestra was playing 'Begin the Beguine', or at least a comprehensible melody from the comforting Cole Porter era.

'I can see for one thing you are an Englishman,' the girl smiled with teeth that defied the darkness. 'An English detective, I think so. Do you know how I tell? You wear a hat. An Englishman is always wearing a hat, most especially is an English detective.'

'And what do you suppose I am investigating?'

'That I cannot be so sure,' the girl giggled with a becoming down turn of the eyes. Even in the muted lantern light he could see that her lashes would outscore any swaggering blond 'Miss America', or 'Miss Australia' for that matter. 'Perhaps it is a handbag or very valuable painting, or perhaps it is a box of ashes.'

James deliberately changed the subject. 'Tell me about yourself.'

'My name is Isha. You are perhaps seeing me; I am running for Japan in the Olympics of '84.'

'A genuine athlete.' James spoke with admiration. 'Would it be rude to enquire what brought you to this?' His eyes rested for a second on the girl's tawdry apparel, or lack of it; then they were discreetly averted.

'You know you do not win so much money if you are not gaining at least Bronze. They tell there is this great Australian patron of sport who will let me run and run and not to go hungry. They say you get good care and good stadiums with Mr Ernest Tyburn. I do not know it mean that I will be obliged day after day to watch this clicket, and also to run onto the track in a way that is not Olympic code.' There was no smile in the girl's voice now. 'You know I wish to run away,' she confessed, 'because this is not sport, this is not how I must win money; but they tell me I have signed, oh how you say, contlact, contract for three years. They say if I try to run Mr Tyburn will have me shut in prison house.'

'But that's outrageous!' James exclaimed with genuine passion. 'Is there no kind of indecency which this vile man is not prepared to indulge?'

He looked up to see she was smiling again, or rather that her brilliant teeth were again a melon slice in the darkness.

'You know you are reminding me of another Englishman. He was old like you, no I do not mean that! He was English gentleman like you. Perhaps too he had been a detective. Also like you he could be very

110

angry about people he is not approving. His name was Sir Gervase Spooner, are you knowing him?'

'Spooner of Swindon, and briefly of the Palace. How could you conceivably have got mixed up with him?'

'Oh, but you know surely he was great friend of Japan. He was loving our customs and our culture and, also' a coy little giggle, 'our geisha.' She must have seen the look of hurt in his eyes because she quickly added, 'No you must not think that I . . . but when we are returning once from Brisbane Games Sir Spooner is saying all the team must visit him at his house on Coburn Peninsula.'

'On the Arafura Sea?'

'Yes, that house. And you know he was so kind and courteous because he was loving Japan. All his servants are Japanese and his, I don't how you say, his not wife, his friend is also Japanese. Her name is Suki, I think he love her very much. But then you know he is not well. He has bad fever and he is shouting in his sleep, sometimes very cross, sometimes very sad. I remember all one night he is moaning over and over, "I have failed the Emperor, I promised him the Bouncer." Yes, he says the Bouncer, I do not know what he means.'

'No, I wouldn't expect you would, it is a clicket term as you might say; but in the context I must confess it also baffles me. However of one thing I'm becoming pretty certain,' James suddenly stiffened into severity. 'You know a good deal more than you pretend.'

'Of what things, I do not understand!'

'Of missing handbags perhaps, or valuable paintings or even a *box of ashes!*' James brutally rapped.

The light was poor and his eyes were not too good

111

these days. He therefore thrust his face close to that of the girl. He had to be able to observe every detail of her reaction.

'I think right, you are a detective,' she smiled without deviousness. 'And you are right too, I know more things than you let me tell. I know you are Mr James Ball OM from London, and I think you are most interested to find the box with the ashes. And I am also thinking if I can help you find it, you will save me from my contlact, contract with Mr Tyburn. I think if I can help you find, you let me run free.'

'You know where the Ashes are?' It was a pretty face in close-up; but this was not the main reason why the veteran security man stayed glued to it like Garbo's cameraman. He had to be in the position to observe the faintest hint of a lie.

'I told you I am a little clairvoice . . . I'm sensational.'

'You mean perhaps you have a sixth sense.'

'Yes,' the oriental eyes glazed unblinkingly back at him. 'I am thinking if you come with me now we will see . . .' A tiny white hand glistened in the Chinese lantern light. It was offered to him, but it was she who reinforced his hesitation. 'But I must warn you it could be dangerous, for you and also for me. If we are found they will think me, excuse the word is difficult, a betlayer. And I must tell you I am a little afraid. Yes of Mr Tyburn but also of his Charlene. She is very beautiful, very sexy person, but also she is very bad temper, very cruel. I do not know what she would do if we are being seen. But if you are trusting me and are not afraid, then let us go very softly and see what perhaps we find.'

James felt the little hand in the palm of his own and decided he must trust her. And so he followed her back to the noisy, illuminated mansion of many architectural styles. An almost bare back, a satined bum shimmying poignantly in the party lights. Again he wished she had been wearing a kimono.

A Glimpse of the Chalice

'I will show you fear in a handful of dust.' It was a line of Eliot's, not Keats's, that slid into James's mind as they climbed a winding staircase undiscovered by any other guest.

'You are stepping too heavily,' the girl Isha hissed on perhaps the two hundredth step. 'You must be very quiet because now we are very close!'

Only a dozen or so steps later the staircase came to a merciful end against a wall of darkness. James heard the minutest click and saw a shaft of light widen sufficiently to admit them both to what appeared to be a kind of minstrel's gallery, executed in the Renaissance style.

But it was below them that the interest lay. Assembled there was a cast of characters he had observed only once before, through binoculars at a travesty of a cricket match. At the centre of the group, further foreshortened by the height, was a toad of a man, half sunken in a wing-collar and smoking jacket. At his side, perhaps head and shoulders above him, stood the dwarf's 'Snow White', at least this was the shade of her moulded ball gown. There was, in fact, little of the fairy tale heroine's simplicity about this white lady, for she was wearing a coronet that seemed to shimmer with the refraction of real diamonds, as did the rockery of stones around her neck. From this angle it was clear, even without the best of sight, that the cut of her ball gown was outrageous. Instinctively, James averted his eyes from the depths of exposure it could never be an interloper's business to explore. They had penetrated Ernie Tyburn's most private of suites.

Stationed around Tyburn and the woman Charlene stood the now familiar squad of thugs dressed as Megatest officials. The group was completed by a bulky man wearing what was perhaps a too rapidly hired dinner jacket and an extremely fat woman of late middle age embedded in a sofa with a small tankard of *crème de menthe*.

'That Mrs Ernie, the wife,' Isha hissed. 'She not go away, though always he is looking at the Charlene.'

'And the gentleman who would perhaps have been advised to consult Moss Bros?'

The girl put her finger to her lips, her eyes imploring silence. But now James had his answer. The man in the ill-fitting jacket had turned momentarily into profile. James had seen this profile before, behind a stack of camera equipment through a good half of a flight to Australia. The bulky man standing with Tyburn at the centre of the group was the American cricket enthusiast Steve Burbek from Newark, New Jersey.

As his eyes began to focus he noticed another thing; two of Tyburn's heavies had automatic pistols trained on the American's stomach.

'I don't like snoopers, Mr Burbek,' Ernie Tyburn was informing him. 'As you will have seen, I am a hospitable man. My doors are open to the highest and the lowest in the land. But you have chosen to abuse my hospitality. Not satisfied with the fabulous selection of refreshments and buffet eats I have outlaid on this function, you have indulged your curiosity to

115

limits that are not courteous, Mr Burbek. And that was wrong of you. Don't I always say to you fellas,' the bulging, malevolent eyes made a quick tour of his henchmen, 'if you want anything of Ernie you've only got to ask.'

A roar of agreement echoed around the tapestried walls of the Renaissance private suite below them.

'Now I understand from the tape of your preliminary interrogation that you, Mr Burbek, are interested in a little object de art previously housed in the MCC Pavilion at Lord's, England and now popularly believed to be in safe keeping somewhere in Australia, its rightful home. But the question you want an answer to is, do I have it? No doubt you've read the speculation in the international media; no doubt you've seen reports of my now famous interview with Michael Parkinson when I insisted that the Ashes belonged by sacred perogative here in our motherland. So you deduced you should pursue your investigations in the privacy of my hearth and home.'

'Don't play with me, you bastards!' Steve Burbek yelled.

'Leave him alone, fellows!' Tyburn rasped, then continued in a silkier tone. 'Just why you should be interested in this historic cricket talisman I confess puzzles me, because you give every appearance of being a gentleman from the United States of America, a country where they won't even pay to watch a Super-powers Megatest!'

'I told you, you zombies, I'm a goddamn cricket nut. I buy the green bonnet!'

'Or maybe, Mr Burbek, you are from a private investigation agency acting on behalf of the fucking poms!' the American's host spat back. 'However that is not the question, is it Mr Burbek?' he continued in a milder tone. 'You want to know if I hold the coveted Ashes, and I'm saying wouldn't it have been more courteous to ask me personally? What do I always tell them?'

'You've only got to ask Ernie!' the muscular Megatest officials boomed.

'Exactly,' grinned the mega millionaire as a Gallipoli canvas by Noland swung sideways to reveal a private safe. 'You see what I mean by trust Mr Burbek. Well, you only have to ask me nicely and I'll answer all your questions.' Tyburn moved with deliberate sluggishness towards the safe and turned slowly to his guest with an upheld bunch of keys. 'What's your guess Mr Burbek. Yes? Or no?'

The tension was becoming oppressive, not least among the secret watchers in the gallery. James felt Isha's small hand tighten into a vice-like grip on his hand and somewhere he thought he heard a stifled sneeze.

Tyburn had been making a lot of play with the locks. Now the door of the safe suddenly swung open, simultaneously triggering a frame of display lighting. Now even James had to gasp because he was looking at a rosewood urn, glowing with mystery and legend. The Ashes!

He watched Burbek at first recoil from the spectacle, then advance with outstretched hand, like a man at the end of a long journey. The American's pudgy hand closed around the priceless trophy. A green flash, fast as electricity. A hideous scream and suddenly the American was thrashing into unconsciousness on the floor, and the flash of green was snaking away across the carpet.

'And it was only one of our harmless grass snakes,' Ernie Tyburn chuckled at his circle. 'No snake bite.

No hint of poison. Merely evidence of a severe coronary. Better if it was fatal. Fill him up with liquor and throw him in one of the pools. I don't like snoopers,' he re-emphasised.

The man was a near dwarf, but the evil of him seemed to grow with every second that passed. It had become a giant and almost physical presence, and in this sense Tyburn could be said to completely dominate the grotesque proceedings unfolding in the tapestried suite. Nevertheless it was the woman Charlene who arrested James's attention. As Burbek was sinking screaming to the carpet from the supposed snake bite, he saw her seize the Ashes Urn from the safe. At first it seemed that she was waving the trophy at the unfortunate American in a gesture of vindictive triumph. But then it became apparent that she was trying to wrestle the lid open, that for some reason she was impatient to examine the contents which everyone knew were merely the ashes of a cricket stump, bail or conceivably ball barbecued by Miss Florrie Morphy of Sunbury, Victoria in honour of her future husband the eighth Earl of Darnley.

She had not noticed that one of Tyburn's bodyguards had noticed her. For a split second the pouting, arrogant face had been creased by an expression of fear and guilt so intense that even James, whose sight was not as good as it had been, was able to register it clearly. The recovery was rapid. In another instant the woman Charlene had regained her sultry poise. Almost disdainfully she replaced the precious Urn in her master's safe. But James Ball had once been described as 'a camera with its shutter open', and now his mind retained the negative of a woman caught badly off guard.

James had been likened to other technology than

mere cameras. Sir Hector Bottle in a charitable mood had once compared him to a cluster of walking radar antennae, and certainly this capability in him was now bristling on the alert. For some minutes now he had been uncomfortably aware that he and Isha were not alone in the minstrel's gallery. That stifled sneeze of some moments back. Now his suspicions were confirmed by an unrestrained explosion, sufficiently loud to alert Tyburn's heavies in the room below. Suddenly the minstrel's gallery was bright enough for a performance by André Previn and the strings of the LSO, and a dim silhouette stationed nearer the balustrade had become a man in a grey flannel suit wearing a Homburg that Isha for one would certainly have have associated with intelligence work.

A stranger might have compared the face that was now turned towards Ball to that of a cornered fox or an English middle-order batsman following on in Trinidad. But for James the face was only analogous to one he had last seen in 'the Cage' at Harpenden preparatory to a Berlin exchange with a dissident surgeon. He was looking at his old adversary I. Smirnov of the KGB struggling fearfully to control another tell-tale sneeze.

'What on earth are you doing here, friend Smirnov?' it was on the tip of his tongue to enquire. But Isha, for all her petite size, had already wrenched him out of his seat, hissing, 'We must please go fast!'

There could be no arguing with her. All of Tyburn's muscular officials had now drawn firearms and the majority of them, heads upraised in menacing fury, were embarking on a staircase that led with only a few twists to the gallery. And somewhere an alarm system was braying.

'Snoopers!' Ernie Tyburn was howling.

Headlong down the secret staircase. And now James was almost flying over Isha on the step below him, because she had suddenly checked herself.

'Listen, they are climbing from below.'

'Then we are trapped!'

'I think so yes.'

'The least I can do is to tell them I forced you up here,' James sighed with resigned gallantry.

'Light breaks where no sun shines,' another poet, a Glamorgan supporter as it happened, had written. And it was at a chink of artificial light that Isha was now pointing, a shred of hope in an extremely black situation. In an instant she had leapt nimbly onto his shoulders, and now the chink of light grew appreciably in size as the resourceful little oriental stripped a blind from a grimy narrow window executed in the Renaissance style. James felt his shoulders sag as the petite athlete sprung at the exposed window and somehow managed to grapple it open without falling.

'Here is my leg. Now you must climb up!' she panted.

'No, go on. I could never make it,' James answered with realistic chivalry.

Yet now there were heavy footsteps both above and below him. Perhaps it was the admittedly attractive shape of the Japanese sprinter's leg, or perhaps it was those painful lessons learned and still not quite forgotten on the assault course at Norwood under the beady eyes of Major 'Batty' Bateman that somehow gave James Ball OM sufficient lift-off to reach and adhere to the girl's ankle. And still he had momentum to spare to take her hand and squeeze after her through the restricted window to liberation.

They dropped onto a bamboo sofa on a dimly lit patio. In James's case the struggle was now for air, for there could be no doubt that his exertions had proved him to be desperately out of training.

'I think we safe now,' Isha whispered. 'We no longer in his private suites.'

And thankfully she was right. As normal breathing and consciousness began to return, James could see that the patio was occupied by other guests, men and women in pairs, many of them in positions of intimacy.

'Darling, you *are* getting adventurous these days. I hope you're not going to try and tell me that this charming little creature is a monster!'

The voice was Jan's, so was the slightly tousled head that had appeared from behind the back of a sofa on the far side of the patio. James hadn't noticed that his hand was still tightly locked around that of the girl who had saved his life.

Hot Lines

1

'I'm sorry,' brusquely apologised the Australian operator, 'but Sir Hector Bootle says he is unwilling to accept a reverse charge call. He suggests you make the call out of your own pocket and submit the charge with your expenses through the usual channels.'

'Will you kindly tell Sir Hector,' James answered with fraying patience, 'that the security of the realm – perhaps of the civilised world – is dependent upon him accepting this call!'

'Just a moment, caller.'

'Curse you, James, what do you think you're playing at?' a voice finally came bouncing off the satellites. 'I trust you realise that this is my private number you're ringing, and that it happens to be two o'clock in the morning! Some of us still have private lives, remember!'

'I wouldn't be too concerned about expenses, Hector,' James riposted sternly. 'We're going to have to call on Treasury funds from henceforth. I fear the matter is getting rather too big for the MCC.'

'The only thing that I would consider could possibly justify this outlandish call, James, is the information that you have recovered the "Churn", rhymes with Urn! And even then I can't help feeling that any sensible person would send a cable by night rates.'

'Oh I've located the "Churn" as you call it; but that's not why I needed to speak to you urgently.'

'Where? How? Look, James, I want it back here on the first plane. I'm being pestered beyond endurance by that grisly old antique Sir Wilfred Breslau at the Museum!'

'For the moment I think it would be prudent to leave it with the present owner! It's going to take a little patience to extract!'

'That hardly sounds like a triumphantly successful mission, James! Are you telling me you've left the "Mashes", rhymes with Ashes, in the hands of that bestial little brute Ernie Tyburn, rhymes with Thigh-burn – or rather the other way around! In any case I'm getting the whiff of another example of serious dereliction of duty on your part!'

'I want Molly out here on the first available flight.' James decided to get straight to the point.

'I daresay there are a lot of women you want, James, but I would seriously doubt whether at your age you could have them. Certainly as far as intelligence work goes you're clearly well past it!'

'Molly ex-of-files at the Oval. Am I beginning to make the gravity of the situation plain?' James was not to be ruffled.

'You mean the bibulous old bat who solved your last case! It's not on, James; the budget simply isn't there. Besides, if I remember correctly, the old dyke always insists on travelling with her female companion. Can you imagine what shipping out that pair to you is going to cost the Club!'

'The Chancellor of the Exchequer, Hector. This is Government business now.'

While he had been talking, James had been moving a number of scraps of paper around the surface of his hotel bedside console. Crudely torn from a notepad, they suggested pieces of a jigsaw puzzle, although in any combination they weren't compatible. On one scrap James had written the word 'ASHES'. On others, the words, 'TYBURN', 'KGB', 'CIA,' 'ESS' and 'CIS,' and the initials of other national security agencies appeared. On a larger scrap, shifting uncertainly around the surface under James's forefinger were the words 'GERVASE SPOONER – PROMISED EMPEROR BOUNCER'.

'It seems hardly credible, but I must tell you, Hector, that I have evidence that the Rumanian and Egyptian Security Services, almost certainly the CIA and our old friend I. Smirnov of the KGB have a lively interest in the "Churn". You will appreciate, I am sure, that this puts an entirely different complexion on the case.'

'I. Smirnov! If that little halitosis case is still at large it's entirely your fault, James. I told you last time you should have had him quietly dropped off Blackfriars Bridge!'

James had not had time to see what had befallen the ubiquitous Russian at the hands of Tyburn's Megatest officials. He fancied he might have suffered a worse fate than a plunge from Blackfriars Bridge. On the other hand, the record showed that for all his faults friend Smirnov was something of a survivor. In any case James decided it would be unnecessarily wasteful of his controller's telephone account to discuss what was essentially a detail. The point to make was that the KGB was demonstrably involved, and that if they ran anything like true to form they could be expected to reinforce their operation.

'Indeed I would not be altogether surprised', James voiced a sudden inspiration aloud, 'if your old acquaintance the Agent Stephanie were soon to show her hand. You remember, I'm sure Hector, how very near she came to ruining your distinguished career.'

He realised he was kicking below the belt; but he doubted if there was any gentler method of getting action out of his increasingly perverse superior. The reference was, of course, to a testing season of a few years back when England seemed to be facing annihilating defeat at the hands of the KGB. At the darkest moment of the struggle, Bootle himself had fallen victim to the wiles of the notorious Stephanie, leaving James's operation desperately exposed. The affair had been hushed up so successfully that later when the tide had been turned, Bootle had been deemed a fitting person to be rewarded with a knighthood from the Queen. Only James Ball knew the full depth of shameful enslavement to an evil cause into which the Prime Minister's Senior Security Adviser had temporarily sunk. He was calculating that Sir Hector Bootle knew he knew.

There was silence on the other side of the world, then an altered voice growled, 'Bugger you, James, what do you want?'

'I told you, Hector, I want Molly's memory, and I want it down here on the next plane.'

'That's not giving us much time, especially since I understand the old soak is none too steady on her pins.'

'I doubt if you could afford another upset at the hands of Agent Stephanie,' James answered coolly and brutally.

'I suppose you wouldn't have a timetable on you? No, of course you wouldn't. You wouldn't lift a finger to help a friend, you disgusting old stinker!'

'I'm sure you'll find they have one in the Prime

Minister's office,' James answered not altogether helpfully before he put the phone down.

2

It was raining in Brisbane, raining torrentially. The tin roof of the boarding house was rattling like a target for machine-gun fire. Yet the rain was not the object of the landlady's impatience. 'Stop that bloody row up there!' she was calling at Sebastian Gover's thin door. 'If I had known you were a journalist I would never have let you take the room!'

So innumerable Manchester landladies had doubtless shouted at the young Neville Cardus. Not for a moment, Gover suspected, had the great man allowed their ignorant complaints to deflect his mind from the green fields where his genius roamed. Certainly no raucous Brisbane landlady was going to disturb Sebastian Gover at his typewriter in the molten act of creation.

The piece he was currently working on had been suggested by a chance remark overheard on an English county ground and remembered on this morning in tranquillity and a measure of financial need: 'Oddly enough the *Church Times* has no regular cricket correspondent.'

The remembrance of the remark had coincided with a frank realisation that it would be financially impossible to continue to cover the Australian tour after the Brisbane Test unless he could find an additional source of income. There was also the matter of a writer's prestige. Gover was still smarting from his cavalier treatment by the *Observer*, all the more so since he was convinced that his talent demanded the setting of a quality national newspaper.

The *Church Times*, it had occurred to him in a heartening flash of inspiration, could answer both his needs – increased financial security and enhanced recognition.

'Today,' he had written, 'the rain blew in from the Bunya Mountains like a judgement to wash out the first day's play of the Queensland match.

We are earnestly prayerful that a resumption will be possible tomorrow, for the England party are still sorely short of practice and, alas, runs. However the intervention of Heaven provides us with an opportunity to meditate at more length than a normal day's play would allow us on the final composition of the 'twelve' for the First Test at the Gabba, now less than a week hence.

Let us first enumerate our blessings, or rather let us attempt to construct an order of service. 'Now thank we all our God' makes a rousing beginning to any matins, and we shall be looking to Chris Broad to provide the same inspiration at the start of England's innings. On present form we can only hope that Robinson is able to support him with an honest to God performance in keeping with his namesake of the reforming 60s, the Bishop and theologian John Robinson.

Every properly conducted service follows a good hymn with a fervent rendering of the Creed. Unfortunately it has become an article of faith in the England camp that the number three position is a devil of a spot to fill. Here both Gower and Gatting have looked at times as doubtful as unbelievers in the Holy Ghost. Possibly Athey could carry more conviction, but he is likely to be saved for that 'green hill far away' in Sydney.

'If I had known you were a journalist, I would never have let you have the room!' the landlady had chosen

127

this moment to howl, like some ferocious caller from Porlock.

' "The Lord's My Shepherd" is a fitting choice of psalm,' Sebastian Gover hammered on as relentlessly as the rain on the roof, 'but can Allan the Lamb be counted on to bring stability to the number four position?'

'Oh Guy our help in ages past!' might be the title of our offertory hymn. But England will be looking for a sizeable 'collection' at this crucial Brisbane service, and it is possible that De Freitas, an excellent team or rather 'sides' man, may be the one who is ultimately delegated to 'take the plate round' for England.

'If you've got to write home, for Christ sake use a bloody pencil!' the landlady vociferously suggested.

'It is to be fervently hoped,' Gover's inspiration crashed on, 'that a good sermon will be forthcoming from Captain Gatting.

Easy platitudes and breezy bromides will no longer do. As so often happens when England is 'praying' away, a prodigal attitude has crept into this touring party that savours of latecomers to the vineyards with little inclination 'to bear the heat of the day'. Gatting will need to summon up all his latent oratory to fire his congregation into a truly evangelistic performance. He must point unhesitatingly to the eternal torments that will result from permitting Border and Richie to get established. And he must instil in his bowlers the conviction that escape from the inferno can only lie in the selfless application of the sacred principles of length, line and movement off the pitch. Let us pray that when the service is concluded on Tuesday week we shall be able to sing a heartfelt, 'The strife is o'er, the battle won!'

'Pack your bags, drongo!' the landlord's resonant voice was now added to that of his hysterical partner.

Sebastian Gover lit a cigarette and smiled a kind of secret smile such as the young Cardus might have smiled on completing the first of his many essays on the Yorkshire all-rounder Emmott Robinson. Yes, he would pack his bags. Yes, he would be going, at least when the rain stopped – going a long way. From the *Church Times* perhaps to the *Guardian* (this piece was richer in metaphor than anything Frank Keating could cook up), or possibly *The Times*, though of course he would refuse to work at Wapping, or even to Tony Lewis's desk at the *Sunday Telegraph*. As he perused the apostolic words that had just erupted from his typewriter, Sebastian Gover grew firmer in the belief that for him the sky was now the limit.

Molly Again

Molly came out of the customs area on an electric
trolley on which two clearly sober grandmothers were
also perched. Beside her marched the female
companion with the hand luggage and duty frees. She
was looking around the crowd of fathers with children
on their shoulders and raucous females awaiting the
return of their globe-hopping menfolk as if searching
for a culprit of at least war criminal status.

Inevitably her search came to an end with James.
'You bastard! You murderer! You cold blooded killer!'
she greeted him. 'You realise this journey is going to
be the end of her!'

'I am sorry,' James smiled wanly. 'I would not have
sent for you both if it was not absolutely vital for
England, perhaps for the world. I hope they looked
after you as hospitably as they could.'

'Thought you were doing us a favour did you?'
barked the distraught woman with the hostility of the
mongrel dog that guarded that odd couple's caravan
at the Football Club end of the Northants County
Cricket Ground. 'Thought you could make up for all
the piggish things you've done to her life with a cheap
freebie to Australia. No, it didn't occur to you, did it,
that the drinks would be on the house all the bloody
way across? Oh no, it never occurred to you – or
perhaps it *did* – that the poor darling would be forced
to drink herself stupid!'

So Hector had not only delivered, but he must, James calculated, have gone to the extraordinary lengths of booking the couple Club Class. James could allow himself only a second of quiet triumph, because Molly was now tipping dangerously off the electric trolley. It needed a quick reaction on his part and that of the incensed companion to prevent her from falling flat on her face.

'Hello Bally, old cock.' An impressionist's palette of a face bleerily turned to him. 'Nice to know you still remember me after all these years. Very flattering to a lady of my age and habits, you saucy old biscuit!'

'It was very good of you to come, Molly.' James pecked at the mat of perspiration and make-up that was her forehead. 'We have important work to do.'

'Do you personally want to write her death warrant?' the companion spat from the close range of Molly's other arm.

'Oh, here's Jan, how nice,' Molly smiled. 'I'll say this for you, darling: you've aged better than I have.' She put a fist into her eye, dragged a trail of mascara down her cheek and peered closer. 'If you're Jan, I'm a Chinaman,' she decided on reflection.

'No, Molly, this is Isha – Jan is in Brisbane for the Queensland match. It's all right, Isha is working for us.'

'Not on the River Kwai they weren't,' Molly muttered as they half carried her towards a taxi.

The plan was that before booking the arrivals into their hotel, a smaller establishment than The Ned Kelly but a little closer to town, Isha would take the companion shopping for an hour, giving James the opportunity to cruise around the city with Molly alone. It was not the expense of this operation that most concerned James. He was fairly confident that all reasonable expenses would now be approved by Sir Hector, at least if the precedent of the Club Class bookings was any yardstick. Much more problematical, James supposed, were the chances of the companion falling in with the plan, especially since she was now insisting that an ambulance rather than a taxi should have been ordered. It was therefore with some nervousness that he proposed the arrangement, wedged as he was uncomfortably between a slumping Molly and her rigidly livid friend.

To his amazement the response, if not gracious, was in the affirmative. Twenty minutes later he was able to drop the two younger women at the Imperial Arcade in Pitt Street, and watch them walk off towards the bright displays of merchandise. He felt, once again, a pang of gratitude towards Isha. She had given him a glimpse of the chalice and arguably saved his life; but this latest demonstration of loyalty was no less appreciated. Certainly the companion stood in need of a new wardrobe. As she tripped away with Isha, it was noticeable that her threadbare dungarees were still caked with the compost or other types of fertiliser the woman used on her tomato plot by the caravan near the Northants ground.

'We're all the same, aren't we?' Molly chuckled asthmatically. 'We love a young face whoever it belongs to. You're no different from the rest, are you Bally, my old pecksniffer? Oriental did you say she was?'

'Gervase Spooner,' said James.

' "By the light of the silvery moon, I like to spoon . . . " Remember that one, old cock?' Molly hummed, letting her head collapse onto his shoulder. 'Oh you could spoon all right in those days, my little

132

Bally-bee; spoon'er as soon as see her – that's what they used to say about you in Files!'

'Gervase Spooner,' James repeated gently easing her head to the upright. 'Spooner and the Bouncer, that's what I have to know.'

'So after all it's a piece of my mind you want and not my body, eh Bally? It used to be the other way round, didn't it, my little turtle dove?'

'Spooner and the Bouncer. It's important, Molly.'

' "But who knows where and when," ' the best memory ever employed by the 'Oval' lapsed into slurred recollections of Rogers and Hart. 'Come on, where is he?' she suddenly demanded. 'Where's Johnnie?'

'Perhaps after all I'd better take you back to your hotel for a nap. We can talk later,' he sighed.

'I'm asking where's the Johnnie Walker, meaning the whisky ration, you dozy old sod!'

'I don't think it would be wise, Molly. I gather the cabin service was dangerously lavish.'

'Come on, James, where is it? You know bloody well Molly doesn't sing without her supper.'

As the November greenery of the Royal Botanic Gardens crept past in keeping with the pace of the downtown traffic, James reluctantly unwrapped the tissues from a half bottle. 'I'm afraid it's brandy. . . .'

'Australian, too,' some extrasensory instinct told the near blind woman. 'You *are* splashing out!'

'But it says it's four star – "Murray Bridge Four Star".' 'Oh well, buggers can't be choosers, as little Guy Burgess used to say. You know he always had a soft spot for the Japs.'

'Guy Burgess?'

'No, Gerry Spooner. Don't say you've forgotten you were asking about him. Your memory must be getting as bad as mine, my old sweetheart. Now Guy, that was another story. . . .'

'No please – Spooner and the Japs,' James almost harshly implored.

'But then it was his Far Eastern experience that got him the job at Swindon.'

'What were they doing at Swindon, Molly?'

'Oooh that's pretty, isn't it?' She looked up from a second hearty swig. 'Now I know where I am. To think Molly should live to see Melbourne Opera House, in the company of her fancy boy, too.'

Macquarie Street had broadened into the forecourt of Sydney's proudest architectural achievement. It made a breath-taking spectacle, enhanced by a vast bay full of sails as carefree as Mozart arias.

'Swindon, Molly,' said James.

'Top Secret Weapon Research Establishment at Munchip Manor, Munchip Village near Swindon, Wilts – codename QFA,' she suddenly recited in a strangely young, efficient voice, free from all slurring.

'I remember the codename. I do not remember learning what it stood for.'

'Just a set of initials – they had so many in those days, didn't they? Not that you were meant to be any the wiser when you found out what they stood for. QFA for the "Quest for the Ashes", if I remember rightly.'

James's hand tightened on the upholstery of the driver's seat; almost without realising it he took the brandy bottle from Molly and rushed it to his lips.

'I think that was another of the director, Sir Horace Stoddart's, little conceits,' Molly's motivated memory disc whirred. 'He was mad about cricket as well as being a professor. Always insisted his letters were directed to the "Long Room", Munchip Manor, after

134

the place they don't allow ladies in at Lord's. Called his boys "The First Eleven", too. Those really clever scientists never grow up – do they?'

'What were they working on, Molly?'

'Oh look, it's just like the picture postcards, isn't it? Talk about a bridge over troubled waters. . . .'

'It was the Bouncer. They were working on the Bouncer, weren't they Molly?'

'Now, that's naughty,' she giggled eerily girlishly. 'You know the codename is never to be circulated below deputy director level. Get your sticky fingers out of my files, Bally.'

'What was the Bouncer, Molly?' James insisted in a taxi on a blue Sydney harbourside.

'Even Kim Philby never knew for sure and that's where you'd get all the real gossip from. But it doesn't take much to put two and two together, does it, Bally boy? They have a "Quest for the Ashes", they discover a thingummy called "the Bouncer". I'm no Albert Einstein, my pet, but I'd say we were talking about a fire-bomb – a blistering big firebomb. Now be a good boy and pass me back my hot water bottle.'

For a moment their two hands closed over a half drained half bottle of Murray Bridge Four Star.

'How did Gervase Spooner fit in?'

'Don't forget I only saw the correspondence, and listened to the odd rumour – well, I was young enough for pillow talk then, wasn't I? He was the blue-eyed boy to start with even though he didn't like cricket. And that counted with Sir Horace Stoddart. Oh, yes, they overlooked a lot of little quirks in his case – like wearing a kimono to dinner and eating his spam and mash with chopsticks.'

'In those days that could have seemed almost treasonable behaviour.'

'Oh he wasn't a Bolshie like so many of them were, but he did have this fancy for Japan. He didn't see any problem about killing Germans, but he was soft as a baby's bottom on the little yellow men. Sir Horace had this notion of getting the Yanks to test Bouncer on the Japanese garrison on Guam, and that's really when Gerry Spooner started to go moody – wrote a highly confidential memorandum to the DG suggesting that Sir Hector should be removed from his post on the grounds that he was a perverted killer.'

'What did the Director General do?'

'Filed the letter. What else did that silly old dodo ever do, sweetheart, and believe me I should know.' Molly began an earthy laugh which turned into a racking cough.

'So things became uneasy between Sir Horace and Spooner?'

'Well of course, Sir Horace was one of the old school, and Gerry Spooner wasn't exactly. But he did a very good job of pretending he wasn't Australian. We had all these letters from Sir Horace asking us to check with the Registrars of Charterhouse, Oundle and Repton to see if he'd been an old boy. You got the impression he talked at least as posh as someone who'd been at Stowe or Merchant Taylors, and yet there was something about his accent which wasn't quite right – I mean for an old stickler like Sir Horace Stoddart.'

'Gervase Spooner an Australian? But he was knighted!'

'So was Donald Bradman, ducky!' Molly tartly reminded him.

If they had been in an office rather than the back of a taxi James would have been pacing the floor. As it was, they were crossing Sydney Bridge and Molly was cooing tipsily girlishly and the scenic effects were, to say the least, distracting. But had they been on the roof of the Taj Mahal, the slopes of Everest or the top of the World Trade Center in Manhattan, the question would still have had to be asked.

'This may sound a rather bizzare, even eccentric request, Molly; but I want you to try very hard to think if there could be any reasonable grounds for my suspicions that Spooner's treason, and I'm assuming from what you tell me that he was a traitor, could have some connection, however tenuous, with the Ashes Urn at Lord's?'

'Come again, darling?' Molly replied, raising the half bottle of brandy to the arches of a fabulous bridge.

James blushed and repeated the question in a slightly simplified form. Even then it seemed an absurd question to put to anyone, let alone an aging woman awash with free QANTAS liquor.

'Why not?' said Molly. 'After all, they had all the relics down there in the "Long Room" of Munchip Manor, Munchip near Swindon, Wilts.'

'Good heavens!' James whistled.

From the deep vaults of her extraordinary memory Molly brought up a little known chapter of wartime history. The time was June 1940. As the French armies crumbled before the Nazi hordes, urgent instructions had gone out from Whitehall to the effect that London's treasures should be crated and transported with all due despatch for safe keeping to the caves of the Mendip hills. Along with the priceless canvases and artifacts of the National Gallery, the British Museum and the Tate Gallery were crated, of course, the treasures of Lord's. The walls of the Long Room were stripped of such enduring masterpieces as

Tossing for Innings attributed to R. James, *Cricket at Hampton Wick* (or possibly Mousley Hurst) at the time wrongly attributed to R. Wilson, RA, a fine portrait of the former Treasurer, Sir Spencer Ponsonby-Fane, almost certainly painted by W. W. Ouless, RA and *Bathsheba at Her Ablutions* with a cricket match in the background, thought to have been played at a sixteenth-century Dutch school. Lovingly displaced, dusted and wrapped were also the bats of Grace and William Gunn, the ball with which the Indian medium pacer Jahangir Khan felled a sparrow, and the bird's stuffed corpse and finally, and perhaps most reverentially, the rosewood Ashes Urn.

It was now that history took a curious twist. According to Molly, the crates labelled 'The Treasures of the Long Room' had attracted the attention of Sir Horace Stoddart, who had been returning from business in Paddington, on the platform of Swindon Junction.

In spite of strong protests from Great Western Railway officials and LVR auxiliaries armed with shotguns, the cricket-mad Sir Horace had insisted that the crates and their incalculably valuable contents should be delivered to his secret address at Munchip Manor, Munchip. Anyone who attempted to countermand these orders had been brutally threatened with a direct report to Sir Horace's intimate friend, Winston Churchill.

'Oh yes,' Molly recalled, 'we had two files thick with complaints from the Ministry of Works, but those Ashes stayed on the mantelpiece in Sir Horace's "Long Room" for the duration.'

'I promised the Emperor the Ashes!' quoted James Ball in awed tones.

Yet the picture was still far from complete. He had

138

the impression of an eccentric, but possibly brilliant professor dominating a room where younger men worked on a deadly weapon of destruction under the gaze of W. G. Grace, Bathsheba at her ablutions, and the former secretaries and treasurers of the MCC. While on the mantelpiece reposed the symbol of their efforts, an Ashes Urn.

'Think harder Molly – Spooner and the Ashes Urn; what was the link?'

There was no answer, except for the sound of heavy breathing. Molly had fallen asleep. Reluctantly James asked the driver if he would be good enough to stop at the first liquor store.

Recall to Duty

Very slowly, an age-old deposit of sand and coral dust was being clawed away. Very slowly a hand appeared, not too unlike a claw, a hand yellowed by time, made skeletal by the near starvation of decades. And after it a rifle-thin wrist began to emerge, wearing a once technologically sophisticated watch that no longer told the time, and afterwards, the bleached tatters of an olive green sleeve, and then, in a small cloud of sand and coral, a museum piece of a *kepi*.

Sergeant Kami Tak of the Imperial Army was coming up for air. His orders had been explicit. Establish a forward observation post on the island of Jum Jum and await the arrival of the main fleet with necessary troop transports for landing operations in the Darwin area. There had been no contingency plans, no orders that conceived of the possibility that no invasion of the Northern Territories of Australia would not be affected by the early winter (late May or June) of 1942. In fact there had been no further orders other than to await the signal.

Sergeant Kami Tak was not a man to reason why. He had been brought up on the toughest disciplines ever imposed on soldiers, including Spartans. Not for one moment in his forty-five years of reconnaissance for the Emperor had he doubted that the signal would come.

This was not to say that life had been easy on

the Empire's farthest flung outpost. The promised reinforcements of men and provisions had never arrived. Even by the spring of 1942 (September/October) it had been necessary to learn to supplement the diminished rice bowl with rock lizards, diseased seagulls and rare catches of the Jum Jum water-rat. Later, as Sergeant Tak's scouting force was steadily reduced, the hunt for fodder had become even more invidious. Regretful cannibalism had helped to sustain him into the late 1960s, but from then onwards survival had largely been a matter of cautiously boiled seaweed. Only once in the last fifteen years had he been maddened into killing and eating an aboriginal construction worker. Sergeant Tak's orders had been emphatic on this point. No attacks or atrocities on civilians until the signal came.

Now the sergeant blinked in the harsh sunlight. He had not surfaced in daylight since 1971, or was it 73? The watch, of course, had stopped decades ago, and the notches he had carved in the bamboo supports of his underground hideout had become so numerous he was beginning to lose count of the days, months and years. In any case the sun was alarmingly bright – like a near miss from British artillery on a southwards-leading Malayan road.

And yet, as he fixed his bayonet, Sergeant Kami Tak knew he could advance with confidence; because at last the signal had come. Not through the rusted and batteryless radio he kept in his hideout with the long-drained bottle of *sake* to remind him of home, but by the whistle they had promised would sound if other means of communication failed. Three sustained notes then a coda of four. There could be no mistake. The time for renewed hostilities had arrived!

Loping, as he had been trained, from cover to cover,

Sergeant Tak began to close on the source of the sound. He muzzled the pain he was feeling in his under-exercised limbs with thoughts of comrades who might still be alive. He wondered if Corporal Osan and Privates Koje and Nissan might be there at the assembly point. He could not remember them dying and he was almost certain he had not been obliged to make a meal of them.

So it was with a hopeful as well as a ferocious leer that the Imperial Army sergeant advanced out of the scrub onto a green enclosure of grass where natives were working with hoses and rollers. He did not pause to sabotage their efforts with a grenade or a bayonet thrust. His orders were to follow the source of the sound, and in any case no atrocities were to be under-taken until new orders were issued.

Molly Again (continued)

'Wake up Molly, it really is Johnnie Walker this time,' James urged in spite of the distaste he was feeling for himself. He was only too well aware that the former Queen of Files had been drinking without stop for over thirty-six hours. Even though he was offering a reviver of genuine Johnnie Walker, he knew the dose could literally kill or cure. He believed he would rather have been torn apart by a Megatest official than by a vengeful female companion. Yet this was the risk he knew he had to take.

A pudgy hand, sparkling with inexpensive rings, twitched at last into life and reached for the half bottle.

'Where's Johnnie? Ah here's Johnnie!' the slumbering woman broke into a warm, waking smile. 'Remember firewatching on Christmas Eve 1943? The "Mini Blitz" they called it, didn't they? Well, we managed to keep warm enough, didn't we, Bally my boy? And, of course, you couldn't reach Jan to say you were late because she was down in the shelter. Those were happy days weren't they!'

'I wonder what they were doing in the "Long Room" of Munchip Manor in 1943.' James deliberately shifted the area of recollection. He was rewarded by a golden nugget of recall.

'The trouble was the trigger mechanism – they couldn't seem to get it right,' the incredible memory coughed into action. 'At least that's the impression I got reading between the lines. They closed the Manor in the autumn of '44, if you remember. But then you can't be sure, can you?'

'Why can't you be sure?'

'Ooo look. I never thought I'd get to cross Canberra Bridge, and in the company of my fancy boy, too!'

'It's Sydney Bridge, Molly, and we crossed it from the other side only half an hour ago. Why can't you be sure?'

'Because he was killed by the only buzz bomb to fall in the Swindon vicinity. Dead men can't talk, you know. Was it you or Kim Philby or Tristan Field who took me to see that picture? Humphrey Bogart and Ida Lupino, wasn't it?'

'Who was killed by the buzz bomb, Molly?'

'Young Leopold Jardine, of course. Now he really was Sir Horace Stoddart's blue-eyed boy. Not just because he had the same name as the England Captain but because he was a brilliant scientist, and in spite of going to school at Harrow! If anyone was going to crack that trigger mechansim Leo Jardine was the boy to do it, and if you read between the lines it looks like he did on the night of 3 July 1944, but, of course, that was the night when the equations went missing.'

'Spooner?'

'Well he was duty officer that night and he did come under suspicion because of his sympathies with Japan. Soon afterwards they promoted him to Head of Security at Buck House. Still, they searched him from top to botty, never trusted him after that, but they couldn't find anything. They searched the "Long Room" from top to bottom too, but they didn't have any luck. And of course they couldn't ask Leo to do his sums again because next day he was buzz bombed, poor boy. Do you remember firewatching with me in the buzz bombs, Bally?'

James did not wish to remember at this moment. His mind was making a careful inventory of the 'Long Room' at Munchip Manor and its known contents. A picture of urchin boys tossing for innings, a top-hatted cricket match on the field of Hampton Wick (or even probably Mousley Hurst), a biblical *femme fatale* oblivious at her ablutions of the primitive cricket origins that were stirring under her window – no hiding place here!

In his mind he heard alarm bells ringing, envisaged the young traitor, badly shaken at hearing the security staff had been alerted so soon, casting desperately around the 'Long Room' of Munchip for a place to secrete the ill-gotten set of equations. And he imagined how severe must have seemed the expression of Sir Spencer Ponsonby-Fane and those of later MCC treasurers and secretaries as they looked down on him in his dilemma. Even the usually benign W.G. strikingly brought to life by the talented brush-work of Archibald Stuart-Wortley, must have appeared to have been looking at him like thunder. Possibly Spooner's fingers played on the gilt frame of the Archibald Stuart-Wortley masterpiece as he calculated the chances of concealing the equations in a picture. Possibly he even took the painting down from the wall only to see it would be impossible to conceal the equations in the picture's backing without cutting tell-tale swathes into the carefully affixed gummed tape.

Then perhaps, in increasing anxiety, his eyes had fallen on Jahangir Khan's ball and the stuffed sparrow in a glass case. No hope of concealment there. But now his eyes would have travelled to the centre of the mantelpiece and here at last he had the receptacle he needed. A rosewood urn unopened for decades, a semi-sacred object that few self-respecting Englishmen would even dare to touch. An urn that even the most suspicious investigator would not have doubted contained anything but the ashes of a stump, bail or conceivably ball barbecued or sacrificed by Miss Florrie Morphy of Sunbury, Victoria.

'Of course, it's so obvious!' James Ball cried. He had no audience. The driver was conducting a monologue on the architectural riches of Sydney's George Street and Molly had once again fallen asleep. He had been so deep in thought he had not heard the steady drip of a downturned whisky bottle emptying onto the taxi floor.

No more could be expected of Molly's memory today. There was no substitute for her, but James was able to fill out most of the rest. Gervase Spooner had been promoted Chief Security Officer at Buckingham Palace in order to remove him to a less sensitive area. He had held the post without incident until shortly after the Coronation and then retired to the Coburn Peninsula, on the Arafura Sea.

A criminal inevitably returns to the scene of his crime, particularly a traitor with a stolen set of equations he would be naturally anxious to reclaim. Within a year, the Treasures of the Long Room had been returned to their rightful place at Lord's. Was Spooner a member? Was there any record of him applying for membership? Any reports of a man seen loitering by the Ashes Urn? James was making a mental note to cable the Secretary, J. Spriggs, in the morning when a minor news item, which had lain dormant in his mind for nearly forty years, suddenly resurfaced.

At a dinner to welcome the 1948 Australian tourists Sir Gervase Spooner, speaking in his capacity as Chief Security Officer for the Palace, had made the bizarre suggestion that the Ashes Urn should be acquired for the nation. 'We are nationalising our mines, our railways and our steel industry,' he had said, or words to this effect. 'Is it not time to consider whether our cultural treasures such as the priceless Ashes Urn for which our two countries will shortly be competing should not be taken into public ownership?'

James had not attended the dinner, but understood that the suggestion had been greeted with loud laughter, indeed that the distinguished guests had supposed that Spooner had been speaking in jest. But in fact he had been in deadly earnest.

Another dormant memory surfaced: a tense evening with Opposition leaders in the House of Commons had reported that Spooner was using his position at the Palace to lobby Labour Ministers with his plan to seize the Ashes for the Nation. Now he came to remember it, it had taken the personal intervention of Labour Prime Minister Clement Attlee, a passionate cricket-lover, to scotch a scheme which, at the time, had seemed but the hair-brained notion of an eccentric, but which today, in the back of a Sydney taxi, bore all the hallmarks of a man with a valuable piece of lost property to reclaim.

It was time to return Molly to her companion, time to link up with Isha again. Tomorrow could literally be too late for the work of recovery they had to do.

The Ashes Mislaid

1

Time: the small hours. Place: Ernie Tyburn's private suite. The Megatest mogul was working late at his desk surrounded by his intimate advisers.

'The first conventional Test between Australia and England at the Gabba is going to be the biggest non-event of the season, correct?' Tyburn was not so gently prompting the semi-circle of stockily filled Megatest blazers that had formed around his desk.

'Too right, Ernie. We've hired a squadron of choppers to over fly the ground with hostesses three times daily,' an aide reported. 'They say they'll be able to get low enough to give the crowds a good display of thigh.'

'There won't be any crowds,' Tyburn corrected him. 'Every bastard in Brisbane is going to be watching Australia v The Superpowers at the Megabowl.'

'Alan Border could draw a few if he gets stuck in,' another aide was brave enough to suggest.

'You can tell the media we've signed him for Megacricket!'

'Golly Ernie, that's a helluva scoop!'

'I said *tell* them. It doesn't have to be true. Now what about advertising?'

'We've got all the sites round the boundary.'

'I want posters of me with Michael Parkinson plastered right round the bloody ground – their ground and ours. What about air time?'

'We've got every bookable slot on Queensland Radio, Ernie. Pre-recorded Megatest commentaries with a wicket falling every fifteen seconds – just to make sure the drongoes switch off the trad Test and tune into us.'

'Screw radio, what about TV? I want to see Tony Greig and his pitch prodders blasted off the screen!'

'Channel Nine, Kerry Packer, dodgy,' another aide objected. 'He's a powerful friend of old-style cricket, Ernie.'

'He's not going to turn away a spend like ours. I need all the prime time he's got.'

'Live, pre-recorded Megatest super-action replays?'

'That, and some exclusive Megaheadline stealers I'll be releasing during the course of this Gabba yawn.'

'Like you've signed Ian Botham?'

'Like I'm advancing the date of the "winner takes all" single-wicket knock-out final with the Megachance to be the escort of the super sex-goddess Charlene at the Tyburn Leisure Complex of the champion's choice – that's going to keep even Botham on the back pages.'

There were whistles of appreciation.

'And then around about the third day, just in case they've managed to work up any interest in their so-called "battle for the Ashes", I'm going to give them the bombshell. I'm going to reveal *I* have the bloody Ashes! True to my promise, I have ensured that that Urn has returned to its rightful place as an ornament to Australian cricket – *Australian Megatest cricket!*'

Ernie Tyburn was a man of some discretion. All

the same he could not prevent his eyes shifting with a kind of pride towards the Noland Gallipoli painting which concealed the safe in which the rosewood Urn secretly shimmered.

'Couldn't there be problems with the law?' the less diplomatic of the aides objected.

'What problems? What law? I don't answer to pom law. Besides I acquired the item in good faith from a reputable international dealer.'

'They've got Interpol onto those Ashes, Ernie. Plus a bunch of private operators, as you well know,' the least diplomatic of the aides persisted.

'What's the trouble, are you scared?'

'No, Ernie.'

'Well it smells like it. It smells like you've just farted.'

The aide protested his innocence, but the Megatest mogul's nose continued to twitch, and one by one his aides began to emulate him.

'Am I right, is there a funny smell in here?'

'Too right, Ernie.'

'Well, someone open a window and let's get back to business. Where was I? . . . Yes, we'll break the Ashes sensation on the Saturday of the Gabba yawn. Are you sure one of you bastards hasn't broken wind? Ne'er mind – back to business, where wash I where? . . .' Tyburn's speech was slurring; his head was beginning to drop over his desk. An aide moved forward with a gesture of concern, but slumped himself across his master's desk.

An alert observer might have noticed that the private suite was gradually filling with vapour. But no one was any longer alert in Tyburn's private suite. They fell in various attitudes of unconsciousness around a sleeping Chieftain.

150

No one heard the door slide open. No one saw the gas-masked figure slip in, or raised a finger while Tyburn's pockets were searched and a ring of keys removed.

Only later was it seen that the Noland painting was hanging sideways, that the safe was unlocked and that the Ashes were gone.

2

'I have to tell you something that is very sad.' Isha looked up from her raw fish dish. 'The box you are so much wanting is gone.'

'The Ashes?'

'Shhh. You said we are not to be mentioning them where there are people. But yes, Mr Tyburn has secretly offered a reward of ten thousand dollars Australian for anyone of his staff who are finding them. He thinks it is the Fucking Poms who are taking them. He says he will kill them very badly.'

They were dining at the Mikado Japanese Restaurant in Victoria Street, Kings Cross. Isha was wearing an attractive silk gown, James his best Horne Brothers pin stripe; but under the table they were both wearing gym shoes. Up until this moment it had seemed that a perilous night lay ahead.

A part of James had to be relieved, because there could be no doubt as to the physical risk, to say nothing of the punitive athletic demands, that would have attended their planned return to Tyburn's castle. Yet all of his best instincts had to be appalled at this news. Unlike Tyburn he was certain the thief was not English; he trembled to think what nationality he could be, all the more so because Molly had caused other memories to surface in his mind.

He remembered on a flight once to Beirut (or was it Basra?) being seated beside a knighted scientist who had been influential in munitions during the war. 'You know, we nearly had something as big as the bomb,' the knight had confided *sotto voce* over a plastic mug of gin. 'It could have burned everything living on the Isle of Wight, and with a missile no bigger than a cricket ball! The principle was damned ingenious – it fed on atmosphere moisture so it could produce one hell of a blaze. And the beauty of it was that it was radiation-free. Our troops could have occupied and devastated enemy territory with perfect safety.'

'I am so sad for you and also for me.' Isha was looking up at him, her engagingly slanted eyes now moist from tearfulness. 'Because if I am helping you to find the Shhh you are helping me to run free from the contlact – sorry, contract with Mr Tyburn. You are helping me not to be put in prison because I break the signature.'

'My dear, you mustn't distress yourself.' James put out a comforting hand and himself felt comforted from contact with the softer, smaller hand his closed around. 'We must put our heads together and think what we can do now.' He resisted the temptation, despite the candle-light and the dark sheen of the young girl's hair, to implement the suggestion literally.

'You know,' Isha whispered, 'I do not think it is the Fucking Poms. I think it is maybe someone else. Perhaps someone who is much closer.'

'Who, Isha?'

'I am thinking in the last Megatest here in Sydney when I am not being obliged to run onto the track,

152

but must assist the Charlene with the Lucky Mega-ticket Draw in the box. And you know that day Mr Tyburn is very drunk with the champagne, that is the day I think when he signs the Sri Lankan clicketers. All the time the Charlene is making the draw he is tugging at her dress – no I do not mean that, she is not having a dress; he is tugging at the gaiter she is wearing round her thighs. And all the time he is saying, 'Come on, gorgeous, what is it you are wanting? You are wanting a diamond as big as the Sydney Hilton? You shall be having it. You are wanting the Tyburn Leisure Centre in Tasmania? You shall be having the incomes. Just so long as you are looking nicely at me, and letting me without the yawns into your bedroom.' And all the afternoon he is fondling at her like this and asking the Charlene what she is wanting. And one time, when she thinks no one is listening, she says, "You are knowing very well what I am wanting. I do not wish anything that is big; what I am wanting is quite small and would not cost you very much to give to me because it is containing only ashes." '

'This creature Charlene said that?'

'That is what she is saying, but she is not explaining why. But Mr Tyburn say this is one thing she cannot be having and the Charlene is looking not so pleased. So you see, dear Mr Bally, why I am saying you must perhaps not be too sad. Perhaps the Charlene is having the box you are so much wanting.'

'You have no other evidence?'

'No, I am only thinking.'

So was James Ball thinking – of a recent evening in the minstrel's gallery of Ernie Tyburn's most private suite. He was thinking of the expression on the woman Charlene's face as she tried, when the focus of attention was directed elsewhere, to wrestle open the lid of the Ashes Urn, and of the expression of anger and frustration the painted face had worn when she was obliged to replace the relic in the safe.

'Perhaps we should talk to the lady in question,' he meaningfully suggested.

'But she is not here. Now she has gone to Brisbane for the Superpower Megatest where she is being the prize in the Tyburn Leisure Complex of his Choice for the Single Wicklet Megachampion, and this, dear Mr Bally, is where I must be going to run onto track when I would so much wish to be running the metres.'

'And where I have an appointment with the First Test,' James said. He remembered another snatch of conversation on the flight to Beirut (or Basra): 'If we had that bomb now we would be the envy of the world,' his companion, who had been big in munitions during the war, had confided. 'You see, it was a genuinely "clean" bomb. We would have been able to keep an effective deterrent with absolutely no trouble from the environmental groups.' James added, on reflection, 'I don't think we have much time to lose.'

'But we will meet again in Brisbane?' Isha half enquired, half gently appealed.

'I shall be depending on your help in Brisbane, dear Isha.' Again he accepted the poignant offer of that slim little hand.

'But first,' she brightened, 'you must be trying with me a delicious Japanese dessert. Is is called yakiraki. It is a little bit sour but also a little bit sweet.'

'It would be a pleasure,' James assented with a sigh. The night was still young, but for him it was nevertheless getting sadly late.

154

Echoes of Bodyline

'David, Mike, Allan, allow me to recharge your glasses. Oh come on now, the night is still young, a couple more aren't going to effect the old batting eye, eh? Heh, heh heh. Not professionals like you! Phil, John, Ian, Chris what about you? Of course, there is Coke if you want it – I mean the stuff in cans – but this does happen to be very good champagne, and by the way I want you to charge your glasses for another toast. . . .'

It was the eve of the First Test. The England team along with the significant media personalities were being entertained to a buffet supper by the British High Commission in a private suite at the Brisbane Imperial. Making a genial round of the Tourists was the diplomat Sandy Winchester.

'Aren't you slightly pressing the hospitality,' James Ball murmured to his old colleague with a studied glance at the bottles of Armagnac and Bollinger the diplomat was seeking to empty into the glasses of the selected squad for the Gabba. 'These chaps will need to have all their wits about them tomorrow.'

'Come on, James, don't be a spoil sport. Neil, you look like a man in need of a refill!'

'If you want us to make a solid start to the series, I would suggest you ration your generosity, Sandy.'

'Strictly between ourselves, James, we simply can't

afford to win this Test,' the diplomat confided out of the corner of his mouth.

'I'd be curious to know why.'

'You must have read the papers. Surely you've seen that negotiations have reached an extremely delicate stage in the British Leyland Land Rover deal with the Australian Forestry Commission. As you can imagine we're up against very tough competition from the Japs. At the moment we're trading on what remains of the Aussies' goodwill towards the old country; but as I suggested to you last time we met, that's going to evaporate very fast if we start to thrash them in the Tests. And by God, don't we need that goodwill if we're going to flog those old Land Rovers! Greg, how about another drop of the crater as they say in Wales!'

There were many ways in which James might have chosen to reply. He could have deplored yet another intrusion of politics into cricket. He could have suggested to the diplomat that for once he thought of England, thought of the shocking indignities to which English cricket had been subjected in the notorious Caribbean tour of '86 and the bleak ensuing summer, thought how vital it was for England also to maintain something of its self-respect on the international field. He could have asked him how long was it going to take the diplomatic service to learn that appeasement, be it to dictator, president or dominion, simply never pays. He could have asked his old colleague Sandy Winchester what had happened to his national pride, could have prompted him to study the dignified and sober example England's Test cricketers were setting, notwithstanding the dubious blandishments they were being subjected to. It went against the grain to leave all these replies unspoken; but James had an even more urgent matter to raise with the over-affable diplomat.

'Sandy, I haven't asked any favours of you on this trip, but I must ask one now. I want you to use your good offices with the Australian security people to get me a confidential print-out on an actress, or should I say hostess, trading under the name of Charlene.'

'What's your interest, James?' the diplomat winked. 'I haven't met the lady, but I understand she has a gorgeous pair of legs.'

'My interest has nothing to do with her legs; but it could have everything to do with the security of the West.'

'Oh dear.' The diplomat's face suddenly lost its genial flush. 'You're talking about trouble. You promised me you were here strictly on pleasure, James.'

'That was my hope,' Ball answered grimly. 'You must believe me that I need that print-out urgently, Sandy.'

'Look, I sincerely hope this has nothing to do with the Urn theft. I've told you how touchy the authorities down here are on that subject.'

'Ashes or possibly dust,' Ball answered unsmilingly.

'Bill, Martyn, you look like you could do with a top up,' the diplomat called cheerily. Out of the corner of his mouth he hissed, 'Listen, James, we had enough trouble smoothing down the ruffled feathers your visit caused. All the old chips on all the old shoulders were showing only too clearly: "Why can't you trust an Australian investigator to handle this." "We don't need any snooty old pom to teach us our business." You can imagine the kind of thing. We had to swear black and blue you were only down here to watch the cricket. If I pass your request on, it's going to blow the whole thing wide open again. And you know how sensitive things are with our Australian friends just at the moment.'

'Too right – and we wouldn't want to lose that Land Rover deal, would we, Sandy?' James sorrowfully smiled.

'Exactly. Gladstone, Phil, John, you look like men who could do with a stiff brandy!'

James turned away from the mortifying spectacle of an English diplomat trying to compromise his country's chances in, whatever any speed-happy West Indian might claim, remained the supreme Tests of cricket. The official line had been made very clear to him. Forget business, forget the future of the world, go back to what you're supposed to be, an elderly gentleman on holiday with his wife to watch the cricket. Incidentally where was Jan?

They had spent hardly half an hour in each other's company since he flew in from Sydney. A peck on the cheek, a slightly barbed comment on his enforced stay in New South Wales and she was off on what she lightly called a shopping expedition. Then back to their hotel, the Wild Colonial Boy, just in time to change for the reception with no shopping bags and no shopping, merely evasions. How well he knew those evasions!

Meanwhile Trevor Bailey was waving cheerily at him.

The big battalions of cricket commentary had just flown in from England. In a rapidly darkening world it was reassuring to see the genial figure of Brian Johnston, as sleekly beaky as the most pampered bird in Regent's Park, enquiring of the Mayor of Brisbane whether he would like a 'piece of music'.

It was good to see Christopher Martin-Jenkins too, (a genuine whiff of the Home Counties in a Brisbane hotel suite), signing copies of his new anthology, *Great Public School Cricketing Disasters*.

His close friend David Frith was also back down under, talking enthusiastically about his forthcoming lavishly illustrated coffee-table book, *The Complete Pictorial History of Cricket from 1066 to 1987*.

But perhaps the most heartening recent arrival of all was Yorkshire and England's Geoffrey Boycott, officially in Australia as the *Daily Mail*'s special correspondent and as an expert summarist for ABC/BBC's radio coverage, yet hinting, nevertheless, that if the call came he was ready to answer it. Below a smart tropical tuxedo the great man was wearing pads.

James, deep in conversation with Mike Brearley, another distinguished new arrival in the Antipodes, was not in a position to observe or see the minor commotion that was taking place at the heavily guarded doors of the reception.

'How dare you deny me entry,' Sebastian Gover was screaming at his heavy manhandlers. 'I am the accredited representative of the *Church Times!*'

'There's no doubt that Gatt and the team will be wanting to give a hundred per cent to this Test,' said Mike Brearley. 'However at the back of their minds they're bound to have the spectre of this match at Jum Jum and the emotionally testing travel arrangements I understand it's going to involve. And of course, all Test matches are played primarily in the mind. When I was skipper, Mr Ball, I tried to exorcise all thoughts of the next fixture from the team's consciousness. I tried to hypnotise them into thinking that there was nothing beyond the present, and you will remember how magnificently Ian and Bob responded to the treatment at Manchester in 1982. They played like men with no tomorrows. Somehow

Mike has got to persuade the lads that Jum Jum simply doesn't exist, that the boundary of the Gaaba is, as it were, the circumference of their world. I suppose you could call it another facet of the art of captaincy.'

'Mike's right,' said Miles Pershore, the England Manager, 'this Jum Jum fixture is becoming a kind of bad omen with the team; I keep getting deputations from them asking me to get the bloody thing cancelled but, as I told you, James, my hands are tied. Everyone seems to be totally overawed by this Tyrone Marshall fellow. By the way, no lasting damage from that toy boomerang, I hope?'

Wally Ficket bore no physical resemblance to a boomerang but he was wheeling around the reception in a manner suggestive of this dire weapon's flight. That he was an uninvited guest was clear from the fact that two hired security men were seeking discreetly to apprehend him, and that in the doorway an elderly couple wearing Eton Rambler blazers and a small crowd of Derbyshire members and their wives were uncertainly poised. That the ex-Test player and tour guide had been drinking more than usual was apparent to James the moment he impacted with him.

'Pardon my French but do I have the honour of addressing the elusive Mr James Lost Ball? We see so little of you, Mr High and Flighty, I am beginning to wonder if our company is becoming uncongenial to you, if you no longer wish to be counted among our gallant band of Kangaroos. Well, that's all right by us, old son. If you don't want to play ball with us and stand your shout at bevy time that's your business. But what I do quarrel with is the way you're not chipping in with your contacts, how you're trying to keep them all to yourself. I mention this, my son, because it just may have escaped your notice that I'm rupturing myself trying to get my party in on the big occasions. I'm falling over myself trying to pull all the strings I can sodding pull to get my party mingling with the team and the personalities.'

'Excuse me, but you are standing on my toes,' James winced.

'And you're getting on my wick!' Wally Ficket fired back. 'Take this evening, for instance. Here's an occasion we'd all have welcomed a pukkah invite to, a real chance for the Kangaroo party to meet the team in friendly relaxed ambience without yours truly having to wade in and practically drag the buggers out of the pavilion! Now don't you think it would have been a nice thought if you'd told Uncle Wally about your invite? Even nicer if you'd used your pull with the powers that be to get us all in on the action! But no, you've got to try and sneak off on the quiet and pretend you've never heard of me! What's wrong with me, Mr High and Mighty Ball, does my breath smell? Do I wear the wrong tie? Do I look like an AIDS victim? May I remind you that I happen to wear the England blazer, sir, and that I've shared the England dressing room with the lads on terms of intimacy you can never hope to espouse to! Oh yes, I've heard the smears they spread about me and the rest of the squad that played in that Headingley Test. I saw that so-called exclusive in the *Sun* that claimed we only got our caps on account of the fact that the Chairman of Selectors had been nobbled by some sexy Russian called Agent Stephanie. Balls! I got my place on merit and I proved it. Those ten runs in the second innings would have been worth their weight in gold if I could have found anybody to stay with me. So let's not underestimate our Uncle Wally, okay? I've got influential friends too. Only yesterday Bruce French crossed the street to talk to me, yes *he* crossed the street not me! So let's have a little more scouts honour, from now on, shall we Mr Slippery Ball? Let's try and pool our contacts, shall we? Am I making my message clear? I'm saying it's time you learned to play cricket with Ficket!'

With a whispered reminder that this was a 'by invitation only' occasion, two security men put the ex-Derby and England player in an arm lock and marched him bellowing from the suite. James decided it was time to mingle with other guests. In his intoxicated condition the distraught man was now shouting James's name loudly, and publicity was the last thing the veteran spycatcher needed at this time.

Yet one sentence in the drunken man's confused and rambling diatribe had lodged in James's mind, ' . . . we only got our caps on account of the fact that the Chairman of Selectors had been nobbled by some sexy Russian agent called Stephanie.' This chance remark had taken him back in memory to a Surrey lawn some summers ago – to a woman with hair that flamed like a Riviera sunset, as arrogant in her athleticism as she was shameless in her sexuality and a croquet match (his will against hers) that had represented perhaps the severest test he had ever faced. Where was Agent Stephanie now? If I. Smirnov was in Australia (or at least had been when last sighted), it would be surprising if his far more formidable compatriot was not far behind. And yet this modern Jezebel who could bring down governments and compromise chairmen of selectors had yet to show her hand. Somewhere on this deadly chessboard there had to be a piece called Agent Stephanie.

*

'You fellas have been beefing about the killer pace your blokes had to face in the West Indies, but don't forget a few decades back it was your quickies who were endangering life and limb. I'm referring to a series called Bodyline.' The speaker was Ray Hammerton of the *Melbourne Argus*, doyen of Australian cricket correspondents, in conversation in a corner of the suite with a group of English cricket writers.

'Isn't it time we buried the hatchet on that one, Ray?' Mike Watts of *The Times* gently ribbed. 'Besides when all is said and done the damage was comparatively light. True, Woodfull and Oldfield both took hard knocks in the Third Test at Adelaide. But you've got to compare that against Gatting's broken nose, and Terry's broken arm and Lloyd's damaged sight in the 1984 series.'

'You chaps don't read history,' Australia's veteran authority countered. 'Nowadays all the attention is focused on the Tests, but if you look back into the record books you'll see that Bodyline claimed its first victim in the MCC v Victoria Match, 11–15 November 1932. For most of the game Jardine kept his secret weapon under wraps though he allowed Larwood just a couple of overs of fast leg theory, which was enough to settle the hash of a very promising young nineteen-year-old batsman called Ron Marsh. He took a savage blow square on the temple trying to give Larwood the Stan McCabe treatment. In a way you could say that bumper killed him, as far as the game went, because young Ron Marsh never played cricket again. He walked right out of the record books, or any kind of documentation for that matter. Nobody ever heard of him from that day on. I'm getting on a bit now, but if I could ever get round to it, I'd ransack the records

163

to try and find out what happened to young Ron Marsh of Sunbury, Victoria. Did he take up farming or hit the bottle? Did he fight in the war? – he would have been of military age. Is he still alive and available for an exclusive interview? It would make quite a fascinating foot note to the history of Bodyline.'

'Hasn't the whole Bodyline business been rather worked to death?' asked Mike Watts.

'No, it would be a sensation! "Bodyline's Forgotten Victim", it would be an incredible scoop! In fact, it would make a best-selling book!' exclaimed Sebastian Gover who had finally persuaded the security screen that he was a bona fide representative of the *Church Times*. It had taken a bit of doing since he had no papers to prove his claim, and as yet had received no message of congratulations or even acceptance of the thought piece he had cabled them during the Queensland match. No matter. The *Church Times* was a dim candle compared to the dazzling prospect that beckoned to him now. To find and exclusively interview in intensive taped sessions the mystery casualty of Bodyline would put the whole media world at his feet! In only a few seconds a youthful cricket reporter had become a fully grown man with a major mission in life.

Woodfull struck over the heart; the dust-up at Adelaide; the cables from the Australian Board of Control; Jardine unbending; a Dominion exploding. To James, it seemed almost cosy now in contrast to his own lonely and desperate Ashes quest. He turned away from the group raking over old ashes to renew his search for Jan, although at the moment he felt it was possible he needed Isha more.

She was standing with her back to him by the doorway. Had she been there all the time? You never quite knew with Jan. She moved in other ways than normal beings, here one second and inexplicably vanished the next, only to reappear as mysteriously as she had gone. Jan was a tall woman; this and the raised Du Maurier and holder served to mask the man with whom she was in conversation. Instinctively, James lowered his eyes to look for white flannels. Jan could be trusted with any man in the world, barring its flannelled fools. He saw instead a pair of slightly crumpled pin-striped trousers.

'Darling, where have you been?' Jan turned to peck his cheek. In the process she unmasked the florid features of a man in preference to whom James would have faced any new lover.

'Ah there you are! I telephoned all over Brisbane to ask you to meet me at the airport. In the upshot, of course, I had to wheel my own luggage through customs! As you can see I was frankly getting so worried about your conduct that I decided the only thing was to fly down here in person. Jan has been telling me something of your doings, and I can tell you frankly, James, that I'm not all that reassured!' bellowed Sir Hector Bootle, the Prime Minister's Senior Security Adviser.

Test Match with Interruptions

1

At last we begin to glimpse light at the end of the tunnel. There was a time last winter as I lay languishing in a Trinidadian jail, in the company of my distinguished fellow prisoner, Sir Geoffrey himself, when I began to despair for Test cricket. Indeed there were dark moments of the soul when your correspondent began to doubt if he would ever be at liberty to report an England innings again, let alone such a spanking start as Broad and Athey have given to this one!

This morning it was as if the ghostly Immigration Officials who haunt the modern game had suddenly relented and stamped our visas for a morning of pure legalised pleasure.

The writer was Matthew Engel of the *Guardian*, not Sebastian Gover. In fact the young reporter was absent from a sunny press box which had seen England's new opening partnership put on 122 by lunchtime without loss. Gover was in Brisbane Central Library closely studying a faded cutting which read:

VICTORIA
First Innings

W. M. Woodfull c Hammond b Allen	5
L. P. O'Brien c Verity b Allen	45
K. E. Rigg b Allen	1

```
L. S. Darling lbw, b Voce        45
T. R. Marsh retd. hurt            0
```

His finger trembled on the last name. A kind of electric charge seemed to spark from it, a signal that
transmitted itself insistently through the finger and
up the arm to the brain. The message read: I will
make you famous, even legendary. And suddenly
Sebastian Gover was visited by a thrilling vision. In
future the name Gover would speak for itself. 'Ah
yes,' they would say, 'you are the man who discovered
Ron Marsh, the lost victim of Bodyline!' And shyly
they would ask for an autograph or an inscription on
the flyleaf of his best-selling book.

'Have you got an index card on Marsh, T. R.
Marsh?' he asked the elderly woman in the reference
library.

'Rodney Marsh? Yes, we have a fair bit on him.'

'No, T.R. – Ron Marsh of Victoria.'

'This is Queensland,' the aging woman reminded
him, aiming a beady look through a pair of gold-
rimmed spectacles. 'Why don't you try Melbourne?'

'Because I can't afford the fare!' Gover suddenly
blurted out. She was old, ugly and dowdy. Her faded,
flower-patterned dress could well have dated from the
thirties. But there must have been something
maternal about her, because for the first time in
months Sebastian had let his guard down. In an erup-
tion of half tearful confession he told the woman of
his struggle to win recognition for his talent, of his
constant battle to make ends meet; above all he told
her of the hopes he nursed in his new mission to
discover the lost victim of Bodyline. 'Seriously, it
could make me famous overnight!' he screamed loudly
enough to turn every head in the reference library.

'Marsh, T.R. He's not listed here,' the woman in yesterday's flowered pattern reported from a brief scrutiny of her card index system.

Sadly, if not actually tearfully, Gover turned away.

'You could try here,' the elderly librarian called him back. Rapidly she scribbled a message on a pad, emphatically folded it and handed it to him with almost a furtive jab. The message read: 'The Yellow Wombat, Fish Street. Ask for Lindsay. Say Beth sent you.'

2

'We've had a number of interruptions this afternoon,' reported Henry Blofeld to his still drowsing English listeners, 'not from bad light or rain, as you might expect, but from helicopters. Indeed these infernal machines could be said to have played a crucial part in Gower's dismissal by Hughes for only three runs and Gatting's stumping by Rixon a few overs later.'

'Well of course, this kind of thing is calculated to take any batsman's eye off the ball,' commented Trevor Bailey.

'I can't remember any Anglo-Australian Test match,' Blofeld continued, 'where helicopters have overflown the ground so low. Can you, Chris?'

'I've never seen anybody sink so low,' Martin-Jenkins tersely replied.

'I'm not sure if one's allowed to mention an advertised product on the BBC, is one, Trevor?'

'It's bound to be a distraction.'

'Suffice it to say that what we have had here this afternoon is a series of frankly rather intrusive visitations from a competitive organisation. We've had the spectacle of a number of no doubt charming airborne young ladies scattering leaflets on the crowd – though as a matter of fact it's been a rather disappointing crowd for the first day of a Test series – and treating us to an extraordinary display of bare. . . .'

'Leg before wicket! And quite clearly, Henry, his eye was off the ball.'

'And on the leg?' Blofeld queried above the roar of whirling blades.

'Of course, this puts an entirely new perspective on the game,' Bailey yelled. '166 for 4 is a very different kettle of fish from 127 for none!'

'There's a simple answer to this,' Sir Hector Bootle growled from a stand at the pavilion end. 'Shoot the blighters down! They have got an air force haven't they?'

Even before the first helicopter had roared in over the Gabba with its leggy load of scantily-clads to stun David Gower into giving an easy chance to first slip, Sir Hector had been in poor humour. Over an early lunch of lobster and Pouilly Fuisse, he had been savage about James's handling of the Ashes search, so much so that Ball had actually been relieved that Jan was absent again on one of her inexplicable vanishings. At the same time, the Senior Security Adviser had been unreceptive to James's urgent whisperings on the mortal crises that underlay the superficial theft of an antique receptacle. He seemed unable to grasp the disturbing implications of the extraordinary interest the original theft had inspired in international espionage circles, or the even grimmer message the second theft spelled out.

'What I can't understand, James, is that you had the damned Urn in your sights and you did nothing about it!' he repeated, as the spangled helicopter spun away, for perhaps the tenth time that day. 'At least you could have got the MCC and that grizzly old antique Sir Wilfred Breslau off our backs!'

A touch on the shoulder. 'Excuse me, you guys, but can you tell me if Davis Gower is still at bat?' Ball turned to see that Steve Burbek from Newark, New Jersey, had slid into the row of seats behind them.

James was not a man given to exaggerated facial expressions, but on this occasion more than one eyebrow was raised. After all, he had last seen the American unconscious on the floor of Tyburn's private suite, and the impresario's orders had been specific as to his fate.

'At least I guess I haven't missed the both Hams,' the Newark cricket enthusiast blithely chatted on. 'From what I hear those twins of yours can sure hand it out. Understand they're pretty good showmen too – not just a couple of *hams*, eh? Those both Hams can really fill a stadium. Right?'

3

Was it Cardus or Ross who had written, 'Down these mean streets a man must go!'? Sebastian Gover was only certain that this was where he was. A cardboard arrow pointed the direction up two flights of stairs. He knocked at a green door, originally a sour apple shade, never anything akin to the dark green Aussie cap. Behind it, the sound of crooned melody, and occasionally raised voices. He knocked again, more hesitantly this time. A panel slid open and in the vacant frame the lower half of a face appeared, creviced and stickley with grey stubble.

'Bugger off!' it said.

'I'm to say Beth sent me' answered Sebastian.

'Whadywant?'

'She said to ask for Lindsay.'

A pellet of saliva struck Sebastian on his spruce, stubbleless cheek.

'Lindsay don't like your kind either,' the lower half of the face grimaced. The door opened. Gover cringed in anticipation of physical assault. He was surprised to find he was being admitted.

The club room was short on furnishings and fittings. In a corner was a juke box of 1950s vintage, perhaps earlier. Sebastian was not to know it was playing a number by Felix Mendelssohn and his Hawaiian Guitars. Beside it, a tropical plant was spreading not unsinister tendrils. The odour of the place was not part of the furnishings, therefore it will not be described. The centrepiece of the club room was a bar of plywood and timber construction. Here a number of elderly but, for the most part, still physically impressive men were drinking. They had not removed their weathered bush hats. Behind the bar a Maria Montez figure, enlarged by time to bulge from a black sequin bodice, was doing duty. Above her sheeny head was a TV screen on which England was batting out of focus.

'Who let in the bad pong?' enquired the tallest of the bush-hatted drinkers.

'There's a nasty smell of pom in here,' observed his minimally shorter companion.

'Beth said to ask for Lindsay,' Sebastian was brave enough to whisper.

Very slowly the tallest of the drinkers and his

minimally shorter companion set down their Castle-maines and began a measured advance towards the young investigative journalist, still hestitating on the threshold of the club room. As he moved forward, the taller man began to search his trouser pocket – for loose change or something more menacing? Gover perspiringly wondered. At the last moment he was spared the knowledge because a wild shout went up from the group around the bar, and the two big men who had been bearing down on him swung round in time to see Chris Broad on his way back to the pavilion.

The replay came up with every local in the bar room screaming triumphantly as Hughes's fast inswinger crept in fuzzy slowmotion under the Notts' man's bat. The entrance of Gower, fortunately from Sebastian's point of view, kept their attention riveted on the off-colour screen above the heaped blackness of the Maria Montez head.

'Nice bowling, boy!' they approved as Gower fenced at a rearing outswinger. The shouts became louder and more overtly hostile when Gower took a glancing blow on his shoulder and peeled off a glove to rub it.

'Hit him again, sonny!'

'Murder the pommie bastard!'

'Break his arm, Merv!'

'Knock his bastard head off!'

'Crucify the buggers!'

'Gouge their eyes out!'

'Soak the lot of them in kerosene!'

Australia was another country, as Sebastian Gover had had over a month to appreciate. He had visited a number of Australian cricket grounds, traditional and unorthodox. He had heard Australian support for its players expressed in many varied and colourful ways; but he had never heard it voiced with such passionate vehemence, not to say violence.

'So what did Beth send you for?'

Sebastian had already become accustomed to looking upwards to face an interlocutor or would-be assailant in this watering hole of giants. As a result he gazed nervously for some time into thin – or rather thick – air before he realised he was being addressed by a man who hardly reached his rib cage. He was wearing a battered, broad brimmed hat in the style favoured by Sir Johannes Bjelke-Petersen, Queensland's hard-line premier.

'Go on, what did Beth send you for? I'm not necessarily going to hit you,' repeated the wiry little man with a face like a much travelled monkey.

'I am making enquiries about T.R. Marsh – Ron Marsh, the first victim of Bodyline. She said to ask here for Lindsay.'

'I've seen disagreeable things happen to men who were making enquiries about Ron Marsh, and they weren't even poms,' the little old monkey-face grinned.

'Blast their goolies off!' howled the small mob under the TV screen.

'You mean you know him, know where he's living now?' The prospect of discovery and media acclaim had made Gover almost fearless.

'It would be safer just to say I knew a man. Safer for you, I mean.'

'A man called Marsh, T.R., retired hurt at Melbourne on 11 November 1932?'

'It would be safer if you are going to ask a question like that to stand a shout. Mine's a Castlemaine like the rest of the blokes, and by the way, my name is Lindsay.'

173

4

'Now remember what I was telling you over the bevies last night, Athers, old son,' Wally Ficket was calling, a pint of Castlemaine in hand, to Gloucestershire's not-out opener. 'Don't get hung up in the edgy eighties! You've got to put that half ton behind you – don't worry, we'll have a pint on it tonight – and just let the runs come till we've really got something to celebrate! Take an old Derbyshire grafter's word for it, Billy boy, there's no point in chancing your arm when you know your old mate Wally could be setting up the bevies till six in the morning just as long as you get that ton on the board for him!'

Percy Gwynne-Watson was not sitting at ease this second session of the First Test at Brisbane. To start with, he had never supposed that the Party meant to condemn him to watching an entire winter of cricket, not after all the wearisome summers he had put in for the Cause. He had assumed that he had been elevated to a front-line role for World Communism, and as far as he was concerned he had acquitted himself creditably in his first test above the Bay of Bengal. He still had a patch of sticking plaster on his thinning scalp to prove it.

Indeed Gwynne-Watson was satisfied he had demonstrated on that Jumbo flight sufficient Socialist ardour to earn warm comradely commendations and a fresh assignment. But since his arrival in Australia he had heard nothing. No commendations, no instructions. The implication had to be that, for the time being at least, he was expected to resume the part of a 'sleeper'. Yet sleep was proving unusually difficult at this cricket match. The constant interruptions of the helicopters had repeatedly jerked him out of his customary protective slumber, and to the whirr of machinery had now been added the coarse interjections of the courier Ficket who occupied the seat immediately behind him. In addition the weather was unbearably hot. Gwynne-Watson had experienced nothing like it in all his enforced summers at Lord's. All of a sudden, the long-standing and loyal agent of the Party was about to snap.

'If this pair can stick together and we get no more interruptions from Westland,' said Trevor Bailey.

'Or Sikorski!' suggested Brian Johnston.

'We could see England with a far more reassuring score on the board than seemed likely earlier in the day.'

'I must say the authorities here laid on a really splendid luncheon for us.'

'Athey has had his moments of uncertainty, particularly when Greg Dyer came on.'

'Of course they should fly higher.'

'Botham too has played surprisingly responsibly.'

'And our thanks to the Lady Mayoress for a quite scrumptious pineapple pudding.'

'But the point is that for almost an hour now we have been able to concentrate on the cricket.'

'Would you believe it,' said former Aussie opener Keith Stackpole, 'we've got a streaker!'

It was not quite true. Percy Gwynne-Watson still wore his panama hat with the ribbon of the MCC, but for the rest he was naked and free. Around him, detestable cricketers were making half hearted efforts to give chase. They were not adroit enough. Like the great 'Round the Corner' Smith of Sussex and Hollywood, Gwynne-Watson produced a ninety degree turn to skim the wicket at the bowler's end. He did not succeed in dislodging the bails without some pain to himself; but the old Fellow Traveller remained heady with exultation, confident in the justice of his one-man protest against the most pernicious game it had ever been his misfortune to be compelled to watch.

'*Ne passeran! Arriba el pueblo!*' he hoarsely hollered as white-helmeted policemen closed in for the inevitable arrest.

Play was finally resumed and, looking slightly bemused, Athey played on.

5

'What did you do in the World War, sonny?' asked the little old man called Lindsay while other Yellow Wombat members hurled jubilant curses at the departing figure of Bill Athey. They had now been fuelled by two rounds on Sebastian Gover, representing half his remaining funds unless the *Church Times* decided to cable with money.

'I wasn't born in the War. I had an uncle who was an air cadet.'

'That could be lucky for you, son, because, you see, me and the blokes especially don't like poms who were in the War,' Lindsay explained with a twisted smile. 'Ever heard of a place called Singapore, even though you weren't born in the War?'

'They don't play Test cricket do they?'

'They didn't play any kind of cricket in Singapore back in 1942,' said Lindsay.

'Smash their bloody noses in!' urged the drinkers under the TV set as Lamb took guard.

'Least of all the bastard poms playing cricket back

in Singapore in 1942. Those evil, yellow fucking bastards sold us right down the river.'

'Set a match to them, Mervy boy!'

'The Australian Second Division we were, straight out of school and never been kissed as you might say. They told us we were sailing to Libya to fight the Germans. All of a sudden we get a signal saying re-route to Singapore to help the bloody poms fight the Japs. Our CO doesn't like the sound of it. He's heard how the poms have been pissing their trousers all the way down the Malay Peninsula, running like bush rabbits from the Japs. So he signals to pom HQ in Singapore and says can you guarantee you can hold the place at least till we arrive. "Oh rather," they say. "No trouble at all, old chap." The day we set foot on Singa the bloody Japs are running all over the place. We're marched straight into the cage at Changi!'

'Cave his lousy helmet in!'

'Ever heard how it was in Changi, sonny?'

'Really I was only asking about Ron Marsh – T. R. Marsh the Victorian batsman.'

'I said, "Ever heard how it was at Changi?"' As had his much taller compatriot, Lindsay seemed to be searching his pocket for loose change.

'Do please tell me.'

'It was worse than murder, sonny: it was bloody torture. Too right, there was no cricket in Changi in 1942. We blame the poms as much as the Japs for that. Every time there was a quarry to be worked or a death march to be made up the bastard pom CO would say, "Give it to the Australians. They've got tougher hides. They're used to working outdoors." You could say we were just about ready for unmarked mass graves when he showed up.'

177

'Who showed up?'

'He had a lot of names. He'd been a lot of places. What did it matter? – he was a white man. He offered us food and liquor and a chance to save our skins. We didn't owe the poms a thing – remember that pommy boy, remember it well. Nor did he, he had bruises to show it. So you could say we didn't feel much compunction at drawing full rations again and joining the Indian National Army as technical advisers on the march into Burma. Now there are people, especially poms, who call that treason. You wouldn't call it treason, would you, young pom?'

'Oh no, I don't think so. But this man?'

'He was smart. Why blame him for that? He saved our bloody skins. Why shouldn't he have saved his? Got himself smuggled into England by the Nips or Krauts, forget which. Got himself a job in top security. Got himself promoted all the way up to bloody Buckingham Palace, but then the poms can't tell their arse from their knees, can they?'

'Bowl his bloody trousers off!'

'We of the Yellow Wombat Brigade don't forgive easily, sonny – especially we don't forgive the poms. What do you think they did when the Japs finally buggered off and left us to their tender mercies in Burma? Forced us to act as fielders for their officers' batting practice. Kept us in the field for ten bloody days!'

'But this man. . . .'

'Did you hear what I'm saying? – forced us to chase that leather pill day after day in the blazing heat. Never gave us a bat. Never even gave us a bloody bowl! The bastards!'

'His name was Ron – T. R. Marsh, hit Larwood

retired hurt 0!' almost screamed Sebastian Gover in a seizure of inspiration.

'He was smart. He had many names. Even fooled the poms into giving him a knighthood. But yes, you could say he learned a healthy loathing for the pom from a certain short delivery bowled a few years back now at Melbourne.'

'Where can I find him? Would he be amenable to a taped interview?'

'I don't know why I've told you all this,' Lindsay mused under his broad-brimmed hat, 'saving that Beth sent you and I'd do anything for that good woman. Without her ministrations – Beth was an Aussie army nurse you know – we would never have survived those ten days of hell in the outfield, never have been able to stand up to all the shit they threw at us at our court martial. It looks like it's your shout again, boy!'

6

'Altogether a pretty satisfactory day for Australia,' commented Keith Stackpole.

'Any shred of hope for England, Keith?'

'Not much. They won a great toss and they've blown it.'

'To be fair to England, they have had these quite persistent interruptions.'

'From helicopters.'

'And streakers.'

'Not ideal conditions for concentration.'

'They've had a beaut of a batting track, Trevor.'

'However, if this pair can stay together till some-where near six-thirty.'

'And we get a little early morning moisture to help our seamers.'

'Australia could find these helicopters difficult to cope with.'

'A quite splendid tea.'

'Those runs on the board could begin to look a little more impressive than they're looking now. . . .'

7

James felt another tap on his shoulder. 'Excuse me, but is that both the Hams at bat out there? That guy who was chuckered just now – was that M. Berry or Ed Mound?'

'Why,' murmured James in a sudden surge of exasperation, 'don't you drop this absurd pretence that you know anything about cricket, Mr Burbek?'

'Listen! I'm a cricket nut. I buy the blue bonnet.'

'You see, I've heard you say something like that before. In Ernie Tyburn's private apartments.'

'You were there, Mr Ball?'

'Incognito you might say. Incidentally, if you were really interested in cricket you would be unlikely to know my name.'

'Why couldn't I just be interested in collecting cricket curios?'

'At the risk of your life?' Ball grimly enquired. 'I'm bound to say I'm surprised to see you are still with us, Mr Burbek. Of the CIA perhaps, rather than Newark, New Jersey? I believe I overheard our host issuing some rather uncharitable instructions concerning enforced intoxication and "accidental" death by drowning. . . .'

'Yeah, lucky I can take my liquor and I was swimming champ at high school.'

'What are you two talking about?' bellowed Sir Hector Bootle.

'The goddamn Ashes, Sir Hector,' Burbek answered in a new, more aggressive tone. 'Seeing as we're all gonna come clean, maybe you know who's got them.'

'You're presumably talking about the Urn,' the Senior Security Adviser huffed. 'I can't see that it's really any of your business.'

'I guess since I represent a member nation of the NATO alliance it is. Have you got them, Sir Hector?'

'You had better ask James; I'd be very surprised if he can give you a satisfactory answer.'

'Tyburn hasn't got them anymore.'

'Agreed,' nodded James.

'We haven't got them. My intelligence tells me neither have the French, nor the Gips, nor the Israelis, nor the goddamn Gadaffis. You know what that tells me about who has got them?'

'The Russians? James, this is more serious for you than I thought.'

'It's one helluva thought to have to live with. Hot, clean and devastating – and it could be all theirs!' Burbek reached across a pudgy hand. 'Maybe it's just as well we guys finally got acquainted. Maybe it's time we kinda got together to try and save the Free World.'

'I'm sure the Prime Minister would have no objection,' cogitated Sir Hector. 'But there could be some awkward questions from the left-wingers in the Cabinet.'

181

'What have we got to lose?' demanded the CIA man. 'We know we don't have them. All we can do is find out for sure who the hell has!'

The last few words were shouted because of the roar of machinery that had erupted over their heads.

8

Back in his subterranean headquarters under the Brisbane Megabowl, Ernie Tyburn was in an evil mood. He still smarted from the theft of the Ashes from his private safe, not least because it had robbed him of the opportunity to create a sensation by unveiling them in the middle of the First Test. Moreover, he was dissatisfied with the comparatively small number of spectators his helicopter raids had succeeded in driving away from the Gabba. Like some infuriated bomber commander, he had spent the afternoon at his intercom ordering ever more intensive air strikes. Now as the small Gabba crowd continued to be absorbed by Australia's success in the field he had thrown in his ace.

She hung suspended over the field of play on a golden ladder, dressed in a gold spangled scarlet gown. In fact it was only half a gown, because one shoulder, one leg and almost one breast were bare. Her lustrous blond hair streamed in the current created by the chopper blades, but otherwise her poise was perfect. It was clearly by design rather than accident that she negligently let drop a golden shoe.

'My name is Charlene,' she purred into a jewelled loud hailer. 'Tonight the lucky Megatest star will win the chance to be my escort at the Tyburn Leisure

Centre of his choice. Will it be Wayne Rockface, Greg Mountain or Brian Phillpot who is privileged to take my hand and escort me to a luxurious five-course meal in exotic ambience with a full orchestra playing a selection of the world's most romantic tunes? Believe me, I have expensive tastes, but my lucky escort will have five thousand dollars in cash to indulge them. Don't you wish you could be him? The big playoff is commencing now at the Megabowl. I'd hurry round there right away if I were you. But don't worry, *I'll* be there.'

'There is of course another suspect,' said James, as the Mega goddess ascended with a languorous wave into the Brisbane heavens, 'if only we can find a means of reaching her.'

Fielding a Substitute

'Thank you, officers,' said Sir Hector Bootle to the Australian plain clothesmen. 'Just put him in the seat over there, will you?'

'Take your hands off me! Where the hell am I?' enquired the England Test renegade, Brian Philpott.

'In a hotel cellar somewhere in Brisbane,' Sir Hector curtly informed him.

'You're not going to get away with this, you know,' Philpott protested. 'I'm a celebrity now. People want to know where I am.'

'And you're not going to get away with your disgraceful desertion of England in her need,' Bootle finger-wagged. 'I can assure you, the authorities at home are taking a very serious view of your case.'

'You want me to work him over, the two-timing slob?' asked Steve Burbek.

'Not just now, thanks,' said Sir Hector. 'Let's see what a little frank discussion does first. There's no hurry, you see. I'm not dining anywhere special tonight. If necessary we can send out for claret and sandwiches.'

'But I've got a date with Charlene at the Tyburn Leisure Complex of my choice,' cried the ex-Warwickshire paceman. 'I'm leaving tonight by Mr Tyburn's private jet for the Barrier Reef!'

'Not content with money, you propose to betray your country for a common tart!' barked Sir Hector.

184

'Whatever would Hobbs or Sutcliffe have thought of you? I can assure you we have rigorous methods of dealing with unsavoury characters of your ilk.'

Philpott pushed back his chair and started to clamber to his feet. 'Look, I'm not putting up with this. I tell you another thing – I'm not going to stand up a woman like Charlene.' He was thrust back into his seat by the Australian plain clothesmen.

'I really can't understand, James, why you felt unable to call in our Australian friends before,' Bootle confided in a scarcely whispered aside. 'They couldn't have been sweeter to me. Now, Philpott, where are your ill-gotten gains? You have five thousand Australian dollars in blood money on you, I understand. You had better put it on the table.'

'Never!' screamed Philpott as his hand flew involuntarily to his blazer. 'This money is for spending on Charlene. She's got very expensive tastes!'

'Why don't you let me knock the bum for five?' enquired Burbek.

'I am sure,' said Bootle in his calmer tone, 'that Philpott is going to see the folly of his ways and put that money on the table. I am sure that he will take note of the fact that I am on the most cordial terms with the Inland Revenue, and that they will certainly regard this obscene payment as undeclared income meriting total confiscation and a punitive fine!'

'Guess they could even throw him in gaol and let him rot – like that guy you had with the mask,' Burbek mused.

'Well, of course, once your name is brought to the attention of the authorities – as I fully intend to do in your case, Philpott – all kinds of unpleasant things can start happening to one. One tends to find oneself caught for speeding on motorways when one is doing seventy-one and, of course, if one's had half a pint to drink, one can be sure to be banned from driving for life. And then of course there are our friends at the Inland Revenue. At a nod from me they'll reopen your file, Philpott, and go back to the year dot to investigate your casual earnings. In fact you'll find you're never out of the law courts. You'll spend your last penny on solicitors' fees. In other words you better put that money on the table sharpish!'

'I'm never going back to England, okay!' Philpott shrilly countered. 'I've found a fabulous new life in Australia. I'm staying here with Megatest cricket and Charlene, if she'll have me.'

'Have you ever heard of Interpol, Philpott? Well these gentlemen have,' Bootle bellowed as the Australian plain clothesmen pleasantly nodded. 'With Interpol and modern communications, Philpott, you can be sure we have the means to pursue you to the uttermost ends of the earth. Now let's see the colour of your money.'

Three stacks of notes were reluctantly laid on the table.

'Thank you. Now if you'll be so kind we'll have your blazer and your flannels. May I say the fact that they are canary yellow only goes to confirm, in my mind, that you are guilty of bringing the game into gross disrepute.'

The Single Wicket Knock-out Champion was so shocked by this demand that he complied. His true reaction was delayed until the garments had been folded and passed along the table for Sir Hector's safekeeping.

'I can't go to meet Charlene like this!' he yelled, indicating the vest and underpants.

'You are not *going* to see the hussy Charlene,' Bootle

informed him. 'We are giving you a chance to make at least some amends to your country.'

'She gave me this fabulous kiss, and hell I earned it. She promised me there might be more.'

'And if you don't mind, we'll trouble you for your hat. It is hardly very flattering to you in any case. Makes you look like some damned pearly king.'

'I'll write to my MP about this!'

'I have no doubt he's a personal friend of mine. Now,' Bootle briskly summarised, 'the officers here are going to find you accommodation for the night in a local police station. The charge is "loitering in a state of undress". If you keep your nose clean, you'll be released in the morning and you may be able to make an application for the return of your money and clothing. But this will be dependent on your good behaviour and, above all, upon your discretion. We don't want anyone, least of all the media, to hear of the discussions we've had here this evening. Now where's this girl of yours, James?'

As Brian Philpott was blanket-wrapped and removed protestingly from the cellar conference room, Isha slipped in with a rustle of silk.

'I can only dare to stay but a few minutes,' she explained. 'I must be at the airfield to run on runway and kiss with all the other girls the winner of an evening with the Charlene.'

Only a few minutes would be riches indeed in this sordid little room of underhand and brutal decision, thought James as he gazed affectionately at the peach-blossom-fresh oriental girl.

'Tell us, where will this broad keep these Ashes stashed?' demanded Steve Burbek.

'Can we be sure she'll have them with her on the Barrier Reef?' asked Sir Hector.

'If she is stealing them, then I think yes she will. A woman is ... you know, not trusting to leave behind in safe things that are precious to her.'

'So she'll almost certainly have them in her suite in the Leisure Complex,' James theorised.

'I've seen her two times I guess,' Burbek mused. 'She's a well-stacked dame, but I guess her tits aren't so big as she could hide those Ashes in them.'

'No, I do not think that possible, and also you see the Charlene is always wearing very tight dresses, very tight fur panti. If she is hiding them there you would see the bulb, I mean the bulge.'

'That means', said Sir Hector grimly, 'that the chap who is going to masquerade as Philpott will have to get a lot further than the end of that five course dinner. He'll *have* to get into her suite!' He turned to his associate of many desperate adventures on Britain's behalf. 'And that's going to ask a lot of you, James, especially at your age.'

'Me, Hector?'

Up to a point it had been James's plan. At least it had been his inspiration to waylay the winner of the Single Wicket Knock-out Championship as a means of obtaining access to the prime suspect. Philpott, in the original scheme, would have been persuaded, if necessary under duress, to use his hours of privacy with the woman Charlene to recover the Ashes for England. But since the beginning of this subterranean meeting it had become clear that Bootle had taken it into his head to add alarming refinements of his own.

'Well, who else is there?' the Senior Security Adviser demanded. 'Burbek can't do it because he's an American. They'd spot him a mile away. I'm out of court because, let's be honest, I'm a warm-blooded man and the woman, I understand, is not without a certain earthy attraction. You yourself, James, have had occasion to comment on my susceptibility to temptresses of the female sex. So that has to leave you. I appreciate you're not the ideal candidate, but you're nearly Philpott's size and you have played first-class cricket – for Cambridge wasn't it?'

'But, Hector, I. . . .'

'I know, James, you're not exactly a lady killer – well you've only got to see the way Jan carries on to appreciate that. But at least you know what we want and I believe, despite all the gaffes you've made on your mission so far, you've got the courage and tenacity to pull it off. I'm sure you don't need me to emphasise how vital this assignment is for England.'

'For the Free World,' corrected Burbek.

'Precisely. Well, you'd better get into your togs, James, otherwise you'll miss your plane. They tell me that the Barrier Reef can look extremely romantic by moonlight.'

James felt a slim hand slip into his. 'You must be very careful, very clever. I will be thinking so much for you,' Isha whispered. James allowed himself the indulgence of returning the little hand's pressure. In spite of all that Sir Hector Bootle had said, he fancied he had succeeded in winning one young heart.

Day Dream Island

1

It was dark when the plane touched down at the tropical paradise of Day Dream Island and, contrary to Sir Hector's prediction, there was no revealing moon.

Besides, the Tyburn scantily-clads in Polynesian dress were too busy concentrating on the ritual movements of their welcoming dance to look him closely in the face. And it was upon the limbs and shaking torsos of those nubile if inexpert dancers that the media preferred to flash its cameras.

James was able to slip almost unheralded into the waiting Suzuki for the short journey over the coral dust to the hotel. Here, at the red-carpeted entrance, a Polynesian styled scantily-clad slipped an immense floral garland over his head. His knees sagged under its weight and his nose twitched from the scent of the rampant tropical blooms. Long into his adulthood James had suffered from hay fever – a return of the malady could prove fatal now. All the same, he recognised the girl could have done him a favour: the lower half of his face was now effectively covered with vegetation. This and the fact that he was wearing Philpott's glittering trilby well down on the forehead meant he was almost completely masked.

'I have an appointment with Miss Charlene,' he

informed the hotel clerk in the nasal Midlands accent he had rehearsed on the plane.

The man behind the onyx desk was not the conventional hotel clerk. He wore a Hawaiian shirt and a gold chain at his neck and had the suntan of a boiled lobster. He was also smiling leeringly, almost impertinently, but (thank heavens) not suspiciously.

'Yes, Mr Philpott, Miss Charlene is expecting you. She says if you would like to wait for her in the Captain Cook Bar she will join you shortly for our five-course dinner.'

'No,' rasped James, 'I will join her for champagne in her private suite.' He peeled off a number of notes from a stack of the prize money. 'I fancy this will ensure a perfectly chilled bottle of Bollinger '83 and a measure of respect for our privacy.'

'Miss Charlene gave strict orders that you are to wait in the Captain Cook Bar,' the tanned clerk smiled, or possibly scowled.

'Perhaps you would be kind enough to tell the chef to prepare some toast and caviare. I understand the lady has expensive tastes. And this I trust', Ball peeled off another couple of notes, 'may make it easier for you to recall her suite number.'

The accent had slipped a long way south of Birmingham, but the aggressive tactics worked. A minute or two later, James was in a marble corridor decorated with live palms, ringing at a door described in gold embossed letters as the 'Princess Diana Suite'. If the fates are kind, James whispered to his labouring heart, it might just be unnecessary to face the demands of the five-course dinner. The door opened electronically.

A voice called, 'I'm in the bath, Mr Philpott. Where I come from a gentleman waits downstairs in the bar for a lady.' The accent suggested that where the voice came from could not be very far from Brisbane. But Ball was not here on a Professor Higgins errand.

He realised that the creature's unavailability in the bath gave him a heaven-sent opportunity to make a search of her apartment. His hurrying feet were brought almost to a standstill by a carpet of downy thickness.

'Since you're here you'd better fix yourself a drink. You can fix one for me too while you're about it,' the voice invited.

The bar was a kind of pagan altar-piece; but Ball moved instead towards a near shop-window of display-lit precious stones. Not diamonds and rubies, but the treasures of the Barrier Reef – exquisite coral formations, luminous marine shells, fossils and encrustations as elaborate as any Renaissance jeweller could craft. Here, it was just possible a rosewood urn could be secreted almost unnoticed.

'Don't tell me you're short-sighted, Mr Megastar,' the twangy but teasing voice called. 'The bar is over there, on the other side of the room.'

He obeyed, looking for concealed close-circuit monitors as he trudged through the plushy depths of carpet. No monitors. No invisible eyes. Yet he was certain he was observed.

'Mine's daiquiri – no, not that one – that one,' the sultry voice pursued him. 'Don't tell me you've never poured a lady a drink, Mr Philpott.'

At the same time as James found the daiquiri bottle, he located the source of the voice. He had noticed before that the massive reception room, blending South Pacific and Louis Quinze styles, tapered towards a kind of dais of marble and gold fixtures. What he had not perceived was that this dais was, in fact, a form of bathroom, or rather that it was the

192

setting for a sunken bath. This was now made evident to him by the surfacing of a Venus figure, artfully blurred, here and there, by bubble foam.

'You can fetch me a towel too,' the voice commanded. 'It's up here, on the gold rail.'

James took a gold tasselled crimson towel, almost as broad as a theatre curtain, and advanced on the arrogant assertion of female irresistibility under its ample protection, a protection for his true identity but also a shield for his eyes. Ball was no priest, yet he dared not contemplate what a second glimpse of this foam-clad body might do to his immortal soul.

Even then there was the perfume to contend with. Only the devil knew what infernal chemistry he had stirred into her bath salts and unguents. The warm, mercifully invisible body exuded the scents of mankind's wildest and most unfettered dreams. When the scent of her became literally unbearable, only then did Ball adjudge himself to be close enough to the naked temptress to let the towel fall.

He stepped back hurriedly, yet managing not to miss his step on the dais, fearing a pouted invitation to rub her down. In fact, Ball had succeeded in draping the entire woman in the requested towel. It brought him a badly needed breathing space, for the creature was obliged to make a number of adjustments before she regained her arrogant poise. Then she advanced with the towel slung so as to do little to conceal the vivid performance of her sleekly moving body.

'You've brought me flowers. How thoughtful.' She smiled lusciously at the protective wreath of vegetation around his neck. 'Really, you shouldn't have troubled,' she mildly protested; but her arms were extended to receive the floral tribute.

The lighting in the suite was not brash, but it was still too bright to risk revealing the lower half of his face. He decided he dared not release the garland until his fingers found a switch or dimmer.

'Tell me something, Mr Megastar: doesn't a gentleman remove his hat in a lady's suite?'

An exploring hand was already on the rim, when the bell rang to signal the fortunate distraction of the champagne and caviare trolley.

'I like your style,' the woman remarked with a sultry sidestep towards the trolley. 'But didn't they tell you I'm bored silly with all this piss water – and this fish paste! Now why don't you fix me that daiquiri?' she enquired with a devastating glance over a bared shoulder as she emptied the Bollinger bottle into the ice bucket.

'Would you like to order your dinner now?' the waiter enquired, conjuring up two menus of tombstone dimensions. 'The sharks' fins are fresh in. I understand they're very tasty.'

'Yes!' barked James. A face could be buried in a menu.

'No,' said the woman Charlene. 'We'd appreciate a little privacy before we eat.'

James watched the rejected waiter and trolley exit with a kind of pity and terror.

'You look older, less athletic than I remember you from the Megabowl; but that's maybe because you're stooping to fix me a daiquiri. Incidentally, there's no need to be shy about your face. It may not be a Wayne Rockface, but it's manly and it's got personality.'

His back was turned, but he could smell she was close to him. Now he felt her talons on his neck. He handed her her daiquiri without looking round.

'Why don't you go and get changed?' he gruffly

suggested as thrilling fingers played on the nape of his neck. The exploring hands fell away.

'If that's what you wish,' the succulent voice crooned. 'Mind you, I'd be surprised if you'd catch Mr Rockface or Mr Mountain making a request like that. But then you're English, aren't you, Brian?'

'Let's just say I'm old fashioned.' James tried to ease his voice back in years and down the social scale. 'I like to have something to undress.'

'It's your party, Mr Philpott.'

He heard the merest whisper of footsteps. He turned round cautiously in time to see her remounting the dais to a bedroom beyond. It was time for action. Time to remove the absurd hat and free himself from the heavy halter of tropical plants. Time to find the light switch that would throw protective darkness round his identity. Yet here was a dilemma. Ball needed light to continue his search for the object all his senses told him was here in this travesty of taste called the 'Princess Diana Suite'.

'You are right, you know. You really are an old-fashioned gentleman, Mr Philpott,' Charlene called from her invisible wardrobe. 'Flowers, champagne and caviare and you do not even follow me into my boudoir. You know, there are not so many gentlemen like you left.'

Ball froze in the act of easing open the showcase of precious fossils and coral formations. Out of sight, the voice of the temptress had undergone a subtle change. It was still redolent of the lands of the Southern Cross, but underlying the Australian veneer James fancied he detected the accent of Europe – Central or even Eastern Europe. Moreover he had an eerie feeling that it was an accent he had heard before in circumstances of mortal danger.

'But then perhaps, Mr Philpott, you are so old fashioned because you are not so young. Perhaps you are really quite old for a fast bowler and punishing right-hand bat, much older than your Ian Botham, much older even than your Geoffrey Boycott.'

James eased shut the showcase of marine treasures and started on a rapid search for the light switch. If he had suspicions about the authenticity of the voice, it was also evident that the voice suspected him. He had left the search for the light switch too late. The woman had reappeared on the steps of the dais and was descending with panther steps towards him while at the open window behind her a black Pacific Ocean roared.

'Now, Mr Cricketer,' she insolently smiled, 'I am dressed for your dinner.'

It was the dress – if you could call it a dress – that seemed to give the game away. Apart from a gold band at her throat she was wearing only a white silken scarf knotted between her magnificent breasts and a pair of boy's cricket shorts of prep school brevity. It was the costume that had destroyed the good name of L. M. S. Partridge, Chairman of Selectors of not so many seasons ago. It was the same costume that had nearly ruined Hector Bootle's career and his hopes of a knighthood. And it was in the same costume, if you could call it such, that the woman who called herself Charlene had sought to demolish James himself one hot summer afternoon on a croquet lawn in Surrey.

'Agent Stephanie?' he wondered aloud.

'Can you be sure, Mr Ball?' The woman who called herself Charlene spoke now in a parody of an Australian accent. 'Is it not possible that your imagination is playing tricks – that I am only reminding you of a woman you met once in an English garden? A woman to whom you were very bad, very rude, because you were so painfully desiring her.' She was speaking unashamedly in the accent of troubled Europe now. 'Is it not possible, Mr James Bally, that you are only dreaming, only longing for me to be that girl who played with you the croquet in the English garden so that you may beg her to forgive you on bending knees?'

Stephanie had played croquet with him then; this woman was playing with him now. And it had, hatefully, to be admitted that she was scoring points. He had triumphed against the legendary wiles of Agent Stephanie on that Esher croquet lawn, but there could be no doubt that she had succeeded in inflicting serious wounds, including the hurtful question that had returned on many sleepless nights: if Hector Bootle had not sounded the gong for lunch could James have continued to resist her a second longer?

'Well it is your evening, Mr Bally.' A hand touched his ear, then stroked his cheek. 'At a Leisure Complex of your choice you must be allowed to indulge your fantasies. You have my permission to dream that this Australian Charlene is truly your good friend of the croquet lawn. Pretend, if you wish, that you are meeting her again (well, is not this the real reason that brings you?); pretend that this time you are taking the hand of friendship that is offered you, that you are kissing it gratefully, hungrily.' The subtle fingers were now playing on his parched lips. 'Pretend now that you are asking for other little favours and that they are being granted to you, even though you are quite a bad old man. Pretend (it is not so difficult, is it Mr Ball?) that now you wish to protect and serve your good friend and share with her all you are knowing

197

about this so stupid little pot. I can promise you it will be more wise to have these dreams than to trust that little Japanese with no breasts you are making yourself so absurd with. Are you understanding me?' The sultry and hypnotic voice demanded as the devil fingers played lightly across his face. 'One kiss from your good friend, if you ask her kindly, will make you forget all those others who are not so good friends.' The gorgeous, satanic face enigmatically smiled. 'I am the Charlene who can make all your dreams come true.'

Long ago in wartime Norwood a Major 'Batty' Bateman had delivered a lecture on enemy agents of the opposite sex for the benefit of a handpicked group of men earmarked for senior positions in the security services. 'The female seductress comes in all shapes and sizes', the Major's voice had rung through the Nissen hut. 'You'll meet it in furs, pearls, in bathing costumes, in tennis slips and even overalls. It may speak with a broken accent or like your sister from Guildford. It's a deadly species of infinite variety; but there's one thing this pernicious pest tends to have in common and it's this – there's nearly always something *false* about it!

'Many a man in the Service has been saved from disgrace or worse by remembering this little watchword of mine – KEPF, means Keep your Eyes Peeled for Falseness. False eyelashes, false teeth, false brassieres or false hair. I can assure you the discovery that the sultry little siren is not all she makes herself out to be will explode the pest's potency like a land mine.'

Echoes of these sage old words reached James across the years as he reached for the blond sheaf of hair that nestled negligently on his tormentor's shoulder, in a manner suggestive of Botticelli's surfacing goddess, and gave it a savage tug. The fair tresses spun anti-clockwise in response to the pressure and suddenly a mane of auburn hair tumbled out.

'Enough of these games,' James panted, taking the woman by the shoulders and roughly shaking her. 'You *are* KGB Agent Stephanie – she of the hair coloured like a Riviera sunset!'

He saw her lips form into a hissing response and then his head sagged under a vicious rabbit chop. Suddenly a mass of fingers were tugging at his ears, gouging at his eyes, tearing at his cheek.

'Keep your filthy pom hands off her, Philpott!' screamed Ernie Tyburn, for his was the diminutive figure that had sprung from a concealed observation post onto the Englishman's back. 'Your prize entitles you to look, not to touch – you nasty little Birmingham shit heap!' The maddened impresario shrilled as James struggled to save his eyesight, his hearing and his face from permanent damage. 'Your prize entitled you to *wait* for the lady in the Captain Cook Bar previous to enjoying an elegant five-course meal in her company; it did not entitle you to invade her privacy and lay your greasy, foul hands on her, you stinking pile of pom dog droppings!'

Now the hands were tearing at the hair on James's scalp in an area where he could ill afford to suffer loss, 'I've got news for you, bonehead,' the demented Megatest mastermind hollered. 'She's all mine, lock stock and boobs. I own every pubic hair of her! Any dirty perverted mind that thinks different is going to rue the day he crossed Ernie Tyburn's path!'

It was a fight now to retain balance. Tyburn was hammering down on him and the thick piled carpet offered little support for his faltering feet. They swayed around the room in a grotesque kind of dance while outside the Pacific waves cascaded in black and white. Dimly, James became aware that there was another man in the room, a man gripping a vase of a Polynesian or Louis Quinze design. He assumed it was a Megatest official and that his plan was to cause him additional hurt. He was wrong in the first impression, possibly correct in the second. However when the blow fell it impacted with Tyburn. James staggered to the wall, freed of his punishing burden, to see the impresario lying on the carpet among a scattering of vase fragments and, standing over him with an uncertain expression on his face, was a middle-aged man of sallow complexion whom he slowly recognised as Agent I. Smirnov of the KGB.

And then James noticed another thing: lying on the carpet with the chunks and splinters of the shattered vase and the concussed near-dwarf was a rosewood container of about the size of a man's outstretched hand: and fixed to it was a faded obituary for English cricket. Impulsively James stooped for the treasured object and heard the click of a firing pin pulled back.

'Why not let him have it, since you are so clumsy, comrade, to reveal its hiding place?' he heard Agent Stephanie advise. 'There is nothing in it for us, nothing in it for him, except perhaps what a stupid Englishman will call "the sentimental value".'

James needed no further invitation to gather the precious Urn to himself and wrestle open the lid. Agent Stephanie was right – there was nothing in it, not even a handful of Ashes.

'For once, Mr Bally,' Stephanie said to a gilt-framed mirror in which she was re-arranging her dishevelled but authentic auburn hair, 'there is a larger brain than ours at work. I do not include this clumsy peasant, Comrade Smirnov – I mean the brains of yours and mine.' She turned to point at the empty vase James was clutching to his breast. 'I am not accustomed to be made of a laugh by a superior intelligence.'

'Yes, you have significantly failed, comrade, to obtain for the Party the equations demanded,' said I. Smirnov with little sorrow in his voice. 'You should, as your orders instructed you, have maintained closer contacts with me, your superior both in seniority and intimacy with cricketering circles. Nevertheless I intend', a grubby handkerchief wiped at a moist nose, 'to ensure that this mission is achieving at least one result that will earn me, if not you, the warm commendations of our comrades at control. I intend now to eliminate the notorious capitalist agent lackey Mr James Balls.' Once again James was presented with the opportunity to familarise himself with the muzzle of the Soviet Army's regulation automatic.

'And have us both arrested and returned by deportation order without the achievement of our mission?' Agent Stephanie retorted scornfully. 'You of all people should know what a bad cold a comrade can catch when he is returning with failure. No, I will try once again to teach you to use your peasant collective-farmer's brain. We ring, you see, for room service – ' she crossed to a marble phone – 'and we tell them . . . Hello, is that room service? I am telling you that our employer, Mr Ernie Tyburn, is being murdered by the Englishman calling himself Philpott. If you hurry you will catch him now. You'll spot him by the Megatest blazer and canary jeans!' The chameleon voice had become blatantly Australian again.

'I am sorry, Mr Bally.' She turned a curiously affectionate gaze on him as she replaced the speaker. 'I have admired, if not your disguises, your cool brains. And now they will do hard things to them and perhaps we will never be having the occasion to play croquet again.'

There was no question of leaping on her as he longed to, and sinking his fingers into her golden but evil neck. He was covered by Smirnov's automatic and already he could hear shouting from below.

Every expensive hotel has a staff staircase and James, still clutching the urn to him, considered he was lucky to find it, particularly since he could now hear violent howls coming from the ascending lift and the richly carpeted guests' staircase. He reached the ground floor in a clatter of buckets and mops and shouldered a door he trusted would open onto a coral island night. In fact, this door opened into the main lobby. And here, as if expecting him, waited the reception clerk of the Hawaiian shirt and the boiled lobster suntan. Behind him was a committee of waiters, barmen and janitors waving a range of impromptu weapons.

The media had inconvenienced James many times in his professional career of secrecy; but for once, when it was most needed, it came to his rescue. The little group of hotel staff was abruptly swept aside by a crowd of shouting reporters and flashing cameramen.

'Did she give you a kiss, Brian?'

'How would you describe your evening with Charlene, Mr Philpott?'

'Will you be returning to her suite after your five course dinner?'

'Are the reports of a secret engagement true?'

'Frankly, did you have intercourse, Mr Philpott?'

'Brian, what's happened to your hair?'

'Blimey, the experience seems to have aged you!'

James returned an answer to none of these frantic

questions; he merely observed to himself that competitive journalism in full cry can sometimes lose sight of its quarry. And this was momentarily what happened. He could not see that there was much prospect of salvation beyond the hotel's glass doors, but he managed to reach them before his disappearance was discovered. A dark frothing ocean in front of him. Behind him a howling pack, some firing questions and others live ammunition. He could not but be aware that the coral dust around him was spurting with finer powder. And now he heard a roar like doomsday and found himself trapped in a shaft of light from heaven.

'The ladder, the ladder, oh please to hold tight the ladder, Mr James!' he heard a girl's voice calling. The voice of an angel or an emissary of death?

2

'At least,' yelled Sir Hector Bootle from the rear seat of an Australian Navy helicopter, 'we've regained the confounded Urn. All we've got to do is empty a few ashtrays into it and we've got that grisly antique Sir Wilfred Breslau off our backs. But I must say, James, I'm extremely disappointed about the matter of the contents.'

'Sir Heckler,' Isha pleaded, 'you must be seeing how he must have peace, must have rest. Look you see, they are very nearly killing him.' Divine little hands moved benignly over James's bruised face.

'You see, James, I laid on this machine in the full expectation that you'd have something – it's hard to talk privately in this infernal machine – something that would justify the gruesome bill our Australian Navy friends here are going to pass onto HMG.'

'Even she is mystified,' James painfully repeated yet again. 'She talks of a larger brain than both of ours.'

'I must say,' in fact Bootle was still shouting, 'with all due respects, James, you've hardly retrieved what's been a thoroughly depressing day for England. But then you didn't hear the close of play score did you? Border's got stuck in. They're 295 for 2. Still, I suppose you're lucky to be alive. I suppose you've got your little Isha to thank for that. I confess I found her earnest pleas on your behalf quite touching, quite moving. But then, as you know James, I'm a notoriously warm-blooded man.'

'Nothing in it, nothing. Why? Why?' James murmured as he sank, despite the harsh roar of the blades, into a caressing oblivion.

Down Memory Lane

'Oh yes, we had names to conjure with then,' said the old Queensland cricketer. 'Names like Brew and Sides and Bensted and Mossops, and your Abo quickie, Eddie Gilbert. Only took one pace to the popping crease, but he could have it around your ears, too right! They ought to have let him put a few down at Jardine's bastards – in the Tests, I'm meaning. But the Board was a yellow livered lot in them days – some called them traitors – said it wasn't cricket to let a bloody heathen loose on the poms. I'm telling you, sonny, that Jardine's mob weren't Christian. Sidewise, Eddie always knew his place. Never tried to stick his black head into the dressing room.'

Sebastian Gover cut hesitantly across these reminiscences. 'Lindsay says you played against Ron Marsh. Do you think you could give me a brief word portrait of him?'

'Sure I did, but my throat is awful dry,' said the old Queensland cricketer.

Sebastian crossed again to the bar of the Queensland Veterans' hospitality tent. Even though the Castlemaine was selling at a discount price in this corner of the Gabba it was a journey he could hardly afford, notwithstanding the fact that he had sold his precious Olivetti to an office systems dealer that morning. Yet the young investigative journalist was able to fortify himself with fabulous expectations. A cable to a top London publisher regarding his Ron Marsh search had elicited this almost instant reply: 'Find him and we could be talking a four-figure contract. Weidenfeld and Nicolson.'

'Too right, I remember young Ron,' said the old Queensland cricketer after more prompting. 'Victoria came up to Brisbane the October of that summer 'fore Jardine's poms darkened the skies. I'm telling you boy, he was good – outscored Ponsford and Darling, and they got 283 between them.'

'What was he like?'

'Good as young Bradman, I'd say, but smarter. Stylish as the boy Archie Jackson, but stronger. They must have had spies at the ground that day. By the time the Englishmen came East he was a marked man.'

'What do you mean, a marked man?'

'Don't you give me that Plum Warner look, sonny boy. You know bloody well what I mean. Young Ron was a marked man, like all of us youngsters who had the technique to play those scalpers, given a fair chance. Here, I'll show you something to write home about.' Slowly the Queensland veteran unbuttoned his worn and lager-stained shirt. An arthritic finger zig-zagged through a mat of grey chest hairs and probed a purple indentation above the left nipple. 'Bloddy Voce did that,' he grimaced.

'I'm sorry,' Sebastian apologised.

'A thing like that marks you for life. Certain as it marked young Ron for life.'

'He became a spy for the Japanese?'

'There are some of us old warriors who wouldn't use that word, son of a pom,' answered the veteran in a frail echo of the tone of menace prevalent at the

Yellow Wombat club. 'There are some of us as would call that man a saviour.'

'I've got it! So you were in Singapore too? You fought in Burma with Lindsay and the Yellow Wombats?'

'And suffered the consequences – ten days of hell in the outfield under a gruelling sun. A man never forgets a thing like that.'

'Lindsay said he had many names.'

'I told you, he was smarter than Bradman. Ever heard of a pom called Sir Gervase Spooner?'

'Yes, I think so.'

'That were one of his names. Oh yes, he was smarter than Bradman, even than old Warwick Armstrong.'

The young journalist looked suddenly deflated. He had just remembered where he had come across the name of Sir Gervase Spooner – while ransacking the paper for the name of the Sports Editor, he had seen it in the Obituary Columns of *The Times*.

'Find him and we could be talking a four-figure contract' Weidenfeld and Nicolson's cable had read.

Outside the hospitality tent the crowd roared for a Greg Matthews six. It sounded like a ferocious blow against Gover personally, for if he was to find Ron Marsh it was apparent now that he would have to conduct his search in the territories of the dead.

' "Sir Gervase Spooner . . . passed away peacefully . . . at his home on the Coburn Peninsula on the Arafura Sea",' Sebastian wistfully quoted from his recollection of the obituary notice. 'In other words you're telling me that Ron Marsh died last month.'

'Some ways a spirit like that never dies,' mused the veteran. 'Look at Ray Lindwall, "Slasher" Mackay and all the great Queenslanders. They're still with us, still full of beans and fight. Techniques like theirs never really moulder in the grave. They just goes marching on.'

'But Sir Gervase Spooner died on the Coburn Peninsula in October – it said so in *The Times*.'

'Nobody dies if they've got the real pom hatred burning in their bellies – look at Lindsay and his mob, they died a hundred deaths on that murderous outfield, but they're still live enough to smash any pom's nose in. Look at our Greg and his brother. Time and again they said they were through. But time and again those Chappells came back to twist the Lion's tail till it howled for mercy like a wallaby in a man trap.'

'You trying to tell me that in some way Marsh – or rather Spooner – is still alive?'

'For those of us who marched into hell wearing the shoulder flash of the Yellow Wombat, too right he is. He saved our bloody lives back in Changi and we revere his memory, if you like to put it that way. There are not too many of us left now and, sidewise, the youngsters don't seem to understand the fight we put up against these sons of Jardine back there in the War. But we'll still render him the occasional service, like dropping beer crates in the path of nosey poms that have no rights to be here, or cutting down the odd snooper with a professionally thrown boomerang.'

'You still haven't answered my question,' insisted Gover, who, in his few days in his new career as investigative journalist, was already learning to be impatient of evasions.

'Maybe as I've already told you too much,' coughed the veteran. 'Sidewise, my throat is powerful dry.'

'Not a drop until you've answered my question,'

snapped Sebastian with a new harshness. 'Is Ron Marsh dead or is he still alive?'

'That's a question I rightly can't answer; but it's strange that you should be asking it now, because there', he pointed with a trembling stick, 'is a gentleman as might be able to help you, though you'd have to ask him mighty nicely.'

Gover yanked round to follow the direction of the veering stick. It was pointed at two young people and a baby. They were wearing T-shirts with the 86–87 America's Cup Slogan: WHAT'S THE WORLD COMING TO? But then the stick came to rest on a tall, handsome and clearly affluent older man. On his arm was a woman of equal elegance and at least his equal in age, parading a picture hat and summer dress suggestive of Harvey Nichols at its costliest. They had paused to watch another Australian boundary, but now their backs turned as they continued their stroll around the ground.

Gover sprang after them only to find he was kissing the beer-soaked grass of the Queensland Veterans' hospitality tent.

'Like I was saying,' explained the old cricketer as he retrieved the handle of his walking stick, 'my throat is powerful dry.'

Golden Trailblazers

'All aboard for the island of Jum Jum where the girls are so yum yum they'll tickle your tum tum! Sorry, naughty one that!' called Wally Ficket as he led the Kangaroo party across the rain-soaked tarmac towards the waiting DC-3.

The torrential rain had come too late to save England from losing the First Test by five wickets the previous evening. And now it had stopped too soon to wash out the flight to Jum Jum.

James, stooping like one of the wind-bent jacaranda trees which fringed the small airfield, followed the Kangaroo party at a distance. He shared none of Ficket's enthusiasm for this late addition to the tour's itinerary. Rather he shared the fears of his friend, the England manager, Miles Pershore, that much inconvenience and perhaps actual injuries to players were to be expected from an island strip that had never previously hosted a first-class cricket match.

In fact, James's fears were more acute than this. Something in his bones – bones which a colleague in the service had once described as being as 'sensitive as hazel twigs' – told him that graver dangers could be anticipated at Jum Jum than a mere matter of an under-prepared wicket. And there were still deeper reasons for James's reluctance to make the journey to this remote island.

It was to be noted that James Ball walked alone.

Like Percy Gwynne-Watson, now under psychiatric surveillance in a Brisbane hospital while his wife gazed blankly at the white walls of the hospital's corridors, Jan was missing from the Kangaroo party. James had offered Ficket the superficial excuse that she was indisposed. Only he knew that this was painfully far from being the truth. Jan had not been waiting for him on his return from Day Dream Island. Instead there had been a magenta envelope on the pillow on which she must have known he would be longing to sink.

My Darling,

I'm desperately hopeful that this letter is not going to hurt you as much as once it might have done. Since we've been in Australia I've noticed an unusual restlessness in you. Let's be honest, my sweet, it's not like you to chase after Romanian nurses and Japanese runner, well is it quite? I know I'm the last wife in the world who can afford to point a finger; but it has seemed to me that your interest in that pretty little sprinter (did you say her name was Esher?) is becoming rather more serious than a casual liaison. The thought just crosses my mind that you've even fallen in love with the slant-eyed little chop suey. I hope so for your sake, my darling; because it's going to make what I have to tell you so much less groan-making.

James, I've met the most marvellous man, and I'm running away with him tonight. I know I've said or written this a hundred times before and you've always nodded your wise old head and told me I'd soon be back. But this is different than almost anything else that has ever happened in my life, and just because that sounds like an awful cliché doesn't mean it isn't dreadfully true.

He's about your age, possibly a year or two younger, and (I hope you won't think this cruel, my pet) extraordinarily sensitive to what I tend to expect from a man and fully able to cope. It's true he's Australian, but he's more urbane

211

and charming than any of your Whitehall friends and, believe me Bally, it *does* help to be stinking rich.

Oh yes, and another thing – he's unmarried, which, when you tot it all up, does make him a pretty unbeatable combination. So you can say that divorce is definitely in the air; though naturally we'll never ask you to do anything shameful like having to get into bed with a barmaid in Brighton or compromising you with your little Esher (or is her name Leatherhead?).

I don't believe you've ever met him, but I dare say you'll know his name. He wasn't too keen that I should reveal it; but then we've never really had any secrets between us, have we? He's a dear, witty and totally sweet industrialist with all kinds of off-shore interests called Tyrone Marshall.

I promise I'll think of you often, my love. I won't pretend it isn't going to feel a bit of a wrench after nearly fifty years. But if it's true your old heart is aflutter for that little butterfly, you'll possibly have an inkling of the way I'm feeling, which is like a girl at her first Eton and Harrow. So pour yourself a stiff brandy, my dearest one – preferably not the local variety – and try not to think me too much of a rotter.

> Your very loving,

> Jan

PS Please don't try to follow me. Tyrone is absolutely firm about that.

It was a hurtful but also curious letter. Never before had Jan deserted him for a man without experience of first-class circket. As far as James knew Tyrone Marshall had none.

'According to my calculations, ladies, gents and mates,' announced Wally Ficket in the narrow gangway of the Golden Trailblazer DC-3, 'the island of Jum Jum measures approximately half a mile wide by a mile long. Now as I reckon it, that means *intimacy*.

No, I don't mean what you're thinking, madam. Really, some people! No, seriously what this suggested to me is that there's no way they're going to be able to keep us separate from the team. In a playing area this size you've got to find yourselves rubbing shoulders with Mike, Dave, Graham, Al, Philyboy and the rest of the lads – and lifting elbows with them afterwards at bevy time.

'So friends, let's have no more binding or letters to the Kangaroo management to the effect that your Uncle Wally isn't getting you mingling with the stars. For a small extra surcharge, I'm handing you the whole of the England touring party on a plate. So just sit back, enjoy the flight and think up all those questions you're going to ask your idols, because, believe me, there's no way they're going to be able to avoid us on the island of Jum Jum.'

The twin-propeller engines coughed, briefly roared and fell into a growling silence. They were metaphors of James's fatigued thought processes. He himself was only too well aware that his mind had done too many miles, had been subjected to too much stress in too many climates to be counted on for an instant response to the ignition button of crisis. Yet all his instincts and those hazel-twig bones told him that it had never been more essential that his brain should get airborne fast.

Yes, Jan was right. He had certainly heard of Tyrone Marshall. In fact his name was lying on James's lap in the shape of a prospectus for the Jum Jum match where he featured on the front cover as the gracious sponsor. But this, and the fact that he was a man of varied off-shore interests who had stolen his wife, was about the sum of his definitive knowledge of the man. Yet even before the receipt of that desolating magenta letter, James had nursed an instinctive mistrust of the Australian tycoon. To his knowledge, no Englishman or Australian, however powerful, had ever used his influence to insert a plainly self-seeking and disruptive fixture into the traditional ritual of an MCC Australian tour. Alternatively it was possibly a matter of geography. By insisting on this game in the Arafura Sea, Marshall had invited, perhaps unconsciously, unpleasant associations with the last resting place of Sir Gervase Spooner, the dead man responsible for all the gruesome adventures that had effectively ruined the Balls' Australian holiday. Rightly or wrongly, James's bones, or hazel twigs, were telling him that a trap had been baited, and that he was flying into it.

The Golden Trailblazer DC-3 had now summoned up sufficient power to make a taxied approach to the runway. The aircraft's single hostess was already demonstrating the requisite safety routines to be followed in the event of a crash, and the captain was predicting a smooth flight once his plane had managed to climb above the local turbulence and low cloud level. His reassuring message was brought to a close by a brief four-letter word which was immediately echoed by the hostess in the demonstration life-jacket. The plane came to a prop-twiddling halt. The hostess stalked, cursing, towards the passenger door. With the help of an alarmingly inexperienced-looking co-pilot, a young man in a mackintosh was hauled aboard. He slumped immediately into the aisle seat next to James where his soaking garments soon began to overspill onto James's pinstripe.

'They said there was no room at the inn. They said there was no seat for me on the media flight,' Sebastian Gover panted.

214

'You're very wet,' said James with unusual directness.

'Of course I'm wet. They deliberately pushed me into that puddle.'

'Journalists tend to be heavy-handed people,' James remarked, hoping that would close the conversation.

'Hacks with a herd instinct – you've said it.' Gover smiled grimly. 'It's only natural that they should turn on the one man among them with a real scoop, I mean *real* scoop – the scoop of a lifetime!'

' "The scoop of a lifetime." You certainly sound like a journalist. Are you sure there wasn't a seat for you on that plane?' remarked James before he realised he had made the mistake of asking a question when all he wanted was to be left alone with his own bleak thoughts.

'Weidenfeld and Nicolson have offered me a four-figure advance. But that's just the tip of the iceberg. I'm talking about world serialisation rights, film and TV options!' exclaimed Sebastian in his new mood of aggressive confidence.

'Another drug scandal I suppose,' James sighed, as he decided to seem to bury himself in the prospectus of the Jum Jum fixture.

The DC-3 had suddenly managed to claw itself into the air and Gover's response reflected the aircraft's surging achievement.

'Who's talking about drugs?' Sebastian screamed above the Dakota's labouring engines. 'I've located Ron Marsh, the missing victim of Bodyline! I'm never going to have to stay in smelly Brisbane boarding houses ever again!

'It's a fascinating story,' the young investigative journalist continued with something of the Ancient

Mariner's irresistibility. 'It's a story of rags to riches, laced with espionage, treason and betrayal. It's a saga which takes the reader from humble beginnings in Sunbury, Victoria, through war-torn Malaya and Singapore to top secret research in Churchill's Britain and a knighthood-winning assignment with royalty. Add the ingredients of Bodyline and a unique chapter in cricketing history and you have to admit I've got an all time best-seller!' Sebastian yelled in his new, more assertive mood.

The prospectus dropped from James's hands. He said quietly but with an emphasis no sensitive ear could have missed, 'You are not, by any chance, talking about Spooner – Sir Gervase Spooner?'

'It's an epic tale that takes you from Melbourne in 1932 where a promising young batsman, as good as Bradman some critics claim, is blighted in his career and embittered for life by a fast-riser from Larwood. He wanders through the Far East and then to England where he assumes the alias of . . . wait a minute – how did you know?' Gover spun an anxious face towards James.

'I didn't,' James answered, 'or rather I should say I didn't trouble to look. I mean look for a background, a compelling motive. And that was unprofessional of me. But now of course you've explained it all. Gervase Spooner's hatred of England sprang from the fact that his real name was Ron Marsh of Victoria. That short innings at Melbourne, an insignificant statistic buried in Wisden that even I had almost forgotten, could be said to have made the world an infinitely more dangerous place to live in.'

'You're not a journalist, are you?' Sebastian demanded with alarm.

'Whatever makes you think that?'

'I'll kill you if you're lying. I'm serious, I've sacrificed everything I own to get this exclusive.'

'I assure you I have only an historical interest in the late Sir Gervase Spooner and his origins,' James reassured him. 'Thanks to you it all begins to fit. What a fascinating study Spooner would have made for the psychologists if he had lived.'

'But that's just it!' cried Sebastian, and then bit his lip.

'You were starting to tell me something, or perhaps like me you suffer occasionally from hay fever?'

'I don't know why,' Sebastian blushed, 'but I've got the feeling I can trust you. In any case, I've got to trust someone because I can't keep it to myself any longer. You see Ron Marsh isn't dead.'

'But surely, Spooner is? It was in *The Times*.'

'Spooner was just another alias, another persona if you like. That's the pattern with Marsh, at least after the incident at Melbourne. He tends to change identities like a chameleon.'

'You really are beginning to intrigue me,' James murmured.

The young investigative journalist stiffened with pride. 'As a matter of fact, I caught a glimpse of him the other day at the Gabba. A distinguished old man with an English woman on his arm, at least I got the feeling she was an English woman – a kind of Peggy Ashcroft with make-up.'

James smirked like an MCC member watching the Haig village cricket final, or like a man in serious pain. An invisible finger of ice was digging into his spine.

'That's why I've got to get to Jum Jum,' Gover triumphantly explained. 'That's why, now I come to think of it, it was just as well they wouldn't have me

in the media plane, because they would have wormed
it out of me. Forced me to divulge that I've found
Ron Marsh – the missing victim of Bodyline!'

'And who is Ron Marsh these days?' James
enquired with an effort at casualness.

'Well look, isn't it obvious!'

Sebastian Gover's ballpoint indicated the Jum Jum
prospectus on his knee. It hovered over the name of
the fixture's sponsor:

TYRONE MARSHALL

Then the pen began a hurried deletion of superfluous
letters as follows:

T̸Y̸RONE̸ MARSHA̸L̸L̸

'Oh preserve us!' gasped James. 'Tyrone Marshall is
Gervase Spooner and Ron Marsh the cricketer!' He
should have known that Jan never eloped with
anybody who had not worn white flannels.

'What about a sing song?' demanded Wally Ficket.
'Anyone know "She Was Only A Test Selector's
Daughter"?'

James noticed the minimum of response from the
self-absorbed Kangaroo party couple, now locked
together in matching Eton Rambler blazers. So every
couple aboard ought to be embracing, James thought
grimly, for we are all destined for a day of reckoning.

Bouncer

'Hello, nobody told me this was a fancy dress occasion!' remarked Wally Ficket as he led his party past the raised bayonets of Sergeant Kami Tak's squad of survivors of the Japanese Imperial Army. 'Now didn't I say there'd be a call for the odd solar topee or yashmak at some stage of this tour. Pity I left my falsies back at the hotel! Sorry, naughty one that.'

'Silent!' rasped Tak. 'You bad Englishman. You prisoner!'

'Welcome to the island of Jum Jum,' an amplifier boomed from a half completed stand on the further boundary of a patchily green cricket field. 'As you can see, the England party are already with us and are now at fielding practice. We wish them well. Cricket is a new game to us Jum Jum islanders, but we're hoping to give them a good match. We're aware that our batting may not be Test class; however we think you'll find we're impressive in the bowling department.'

'Mike! Embers my son! Davo mate! Guy my old friend!' cried Wally Ficket, glimpsing the white sweaters of England with no barriers in between. 'Get your skates on gents and ladies!' he turned to exhort the Kangaroo tourists. 'This is mingling time!'

The ex-England and Derby man started forward with the ponderous acceleration that had once obtained him a scampered ten in a certain Test at

Headingley. Sergeant Kami Tak brought his rifle butt up and savagely clubbed him. It was fortunate for Ficket that Tak's arms were still stiff from years of concealment in his cramped hideaway, otherwise the blow would have impacted with his skull and possibly killed him. As it was it fell across his shoulders and merely took his legs from him.

'What kind of fancy dress party do you call this?' Ficket asked from his seat in the dust.

Now James noticed that other uniforms were on parade. As he drew closer he saw that they belonged to Australian troops of the Second World War period. Ball had observed these splendid fighting men on many fronts during the war years. These men were different. In the first place they were without exception well over military age. In the second, there was a difference about the uniform. A large shoulder flash portrayed what appeared to be a winged insect woven in golden thread. On the traditional Australian bushranger's hat was an insignia that looked suspiciously like the Rising Sun.

Like the Japanese contingent these men were also carrying their rifles at the port with bayonets fixed. They appeared to have set themselves the task of standing guard on England's fielding practice. And here it was becoming evident that the Tourists were not voluntarily at play.

In front of them a modern bowling machine, of the type used by England batsmen in the Caribbean in 1986 in an effort to familiarise themselves with West Indian pace, had been pressed into service as a kind of canon. A small, wizened man in Australian uniform was loading buckets of cricket balls for rapid fire at the uncomfortable fielders.

'Now, you bastards, let's see you catch this one!'

Lindsay was jubilantly crowing. 'Pick it up, butter fingers. You idle buggers! Right let's see you get your hands round this one. I'm moving the speed up to ninety m.p.h. So mind your fingers! What are you complaining about, son? We took worse from your pals in Burma back in '45. We took ten days of hell from you bastards!'

'The Yellow Wombats!' exclaimed Sebastian Gover at James's elbow, 'Marsh's force of collaborators, recruited from the prison camps of Singapore and Malaya. They are re-enacting the field punishment that was handed out to them by their British captors in Burma, only this time the roles are reversed!'

'Ah, James, good to see you looking fit and well,' Sandy Winchester strolled past with a touch of his sun hat. It carried the legend: 'Jum Jum, Island of Sunshine and Cricket'. 'We've got a beautiful day for it, haven't we? Going to do us a power of good in a region where we badly need to make friends.'

'Sandy, you've got to find a telephone and call the High Commission in Canberra now. Tell them,' James insisted, 'that if help doesn't arrive in the next hour. . . .'

'I don't want to sound rude, James, but have you caught a spot of the sun?'

'Look around you, you idiotic old appeaser,' James spat out in exasperation. 'Japanese soldiers clubbing English citizens in broad daylight! Australian quislings pointing rifles at our men! Can't you see that we're in desperate . . . ?'

'May I have your attention, please.' The amplifier erased the rest of James's urgent plea. 'Very soon we will be commencing play in the first, and possibly the last, official cricket fixture at Jum Jum. You could say for us natives this is the Final Test.'

221

'Ring the High Commission now!' James called unavailingly at the socialising back of Sandy Winchester.

'In the truest sense,' the harsh amplifier voice continued, 'the game you are going to experience will be a Test Match – a test of nerve, a test of physique and fast reaction, above all a test of the will to survive.'

'I said the TCCB were mad to authorise this fixture!' muttered Miles Pershore, the England Manager, with a meaningful glance for James.

'Implicit in the term "Test Match" must be the concept of a trail,' the amplified voice rolled on over the island's modest playing area. 'So you are entitled to ask who is on trial today. There's a simple answer. If our visitors will care to look around them, they will notice that without exception they hail from the British Isles and in particular from England.'

For no special reason James found himself thinking of Hector Bootle on the fairways. In preference to the Jum Jum fixture, the Senior Security Adviser had accepted an invitation to play golf with Dennis Lillee and Greg Chappell. It had proved an inspired decision, at least for Bootle. In a poignant flash of revelation, James understood why a man like Hector would always be senior management while he, though arguably equipped with an infinitely better mind, would always remain in a lower stratum. Bootle had the god-given ability never to find himself in the wrong place at wretchedly wrong times.

'No doubt being English gentlemen and ladies, you consider your Englishness to be a matter of pride, of self-congratulation even!' A slightly manic note had crept into the hitherto even delivery of the amplified voice. 'I assure you, gentlemen and ladies, you would have felt no pride in your country if you had been present at the MCG on the morning of 11 November 1932. On the contrary it is to be hoped that you would have felt revulsion, outrage and shame.'

'The voice – it's Ron Marsh!' gasped Sebastian Gover.

'Sir Gervase Spooner,' murmured James.

'Or Tyrone Marshall, as he now is,' Sebastian completed the grim deduction.

'You would have felt no pride in your country had you been present at the internment complex of Changi in March 1942. On the contrary it is to be hoped you would have felt disgraced by the arrogance shown by your countrymen to their hard-pressed Japanese guards, and the brutality they demonstrated to the Australian troops they had forced to bear arms in their doomed cause.'

'Too right!' shouted the veterans of the Yellow Wombat Brigade with a flourish of bayonets.

'I can promise you would have felt no pride in your country had you been engaged in the so called "Quest for the Ashes" at the secret research establishment of Munchip Manor, near Swindon in the winter of '43–'44. On the contrary you might have felt everlastingly stained with crime! On the other hand being nice, well-spoken English people who always "play the game" you would, more probably, have seen nothing wrong with the idea of roasting alive the entire courteous, family-loving Japanese garrison of Guam, merely to impress the Americans. Nor, I suspect, would you have had a scruple about unloosing the Scottish psychopath Douglas Jardine to tear the heart out of our young manhood!'

'Too right! Bomb the poms to hell!' bellowed the veterans of the Yellow Wombat Brigade.

'So you see, ladies and gentlemen, or at least visitors to Jum Jum, what we have here today is a trial rather than a Test. You may claim you are innocent of the serious charges that are being brought against you and your nation. I will answer you this. To the England cricketers among us I will say, can you plead innocence when you continue to flout the colours of a club that has never renounced the crimes of Douglas Jardine, and his licensed bully boys? To your followers, I will say only this, how can you claim you are guiltless when you include men in your numbers – the secret agent James Ball is merely one – men who are ruthlessly determined to retrieve the secret of the Bouncer for England, no doubt with the aim of the brutal incineration of more hapless orientals!'

'The man is quite mad!' whistled James.

'He's certainly willing to talk,' observed Sebastian Gover. 'I just wish he'd stop broadcasting his revelations. I've got to get an *exclusive* interview before he spills it all.'

He started forward. James saw a Japanese rifle butt raised and firmly restrained him.

'My dear young friend, you have enough copy already,' he sighed.

'So you see my friends, or rather visitors to Jum Jum, you really can't complain if today we bowl you the odd short one. Nor can you quibble that the Bouncer we've got up our sleeve is an unfair type of delivery – because it is your own fiendish invention! Let me reveal, since we are among friends, or at least people who are unlikely to let it go any further, a little of Bouncer's history.'

'Now it will be in *all* tomorrow's papers,' Sebastian moaned.

'I very much doubt it, the way things are beginning to look,' James coldly comforted.

'It was the pet project of a notorious supporter of Bodyline named Sir Horace Stoddart. He ran his secret research establishment with all the snobbery and ruthlessness of England's malevolent skipper in that infamous series. Indeed, he unashamedly likened his hideous device to the weapon of Larwood and Voce. And was it a coincidence that his favourite protégé rejoiced, or was rather blighted, in the name of Jardine? Mercifully, Stoddart and his team had problems in designing an effective trigger mechanism for their obscene fireball. It was not until summer 1944 that a feasible set of equations was produced. Late, but still not too late to spare our dear friends of the Orient from further grievous suffering! Thanks to the efforts of a young humanitarian named Gervase Spooner, these equations were never translated into military hardware. They remained, until this year, in a secret hiding place.'

'Why, for goodness' sake, didn't you leave them there?' James, usually a quietly spoken man, cupped his hands and shouted at the nearest loudspeaker.

An amplified hesitation and a clearing of the throat answered him. Then the microphones rediscovered their voice – a voice now of unmistakable doom.

'Ashes to ashes, dust to dust. You have sown the whirlwind. It must be reaped.'

'Nonsense!' James defiantly barked. 'You're a mean little provincial, Marsh, Spooner, Marshall or whatever you're calling yourself today – a mean little provincial with an absurd and monstrous grudge against society!'

'I promised the Emperor the Ashes,' the loudspeaker blared back, 'and those who have served His

225

Imperial Majesty will know that was a sacred pledge. However, despite repeated approaches, the Emperor, in his divine wisdom, turned a deaf ear to us, for too long for us to be able to nurse any futher hope of his acceptance. Indeed, it could be said that His Imperial Majesty's clear disinterest was the death of my close friend, Sir Gervase Spooner.'

'What on earth is the fellow going on about?' enquired Miles Pershore.

'Hush,' James motioned. 'We are listening to the exposed mechanism of a deranged and criminal mind.'

'Don't forget he took a nasty knock in the temple at Melbourne,' Sebastian Gover scrupulously reminded them.

'In other words,' the amplifiers crackled into new life. 'We considered ourselves, at last, to be released from our pledge, and able to offer the product on the open market. Now, as our more informed guests will be aware, the Bouncer is not a product suitable for direct advertising. More subtle techniques are required to alert potential customers. An inspired PR exercise if you like.'

'Such as the theft of the Urn?' James demanded with all his lungs.

'Correct, Mr Ball. It secured us world headlines. This, together with a series of inspired leaks as to the Urn's possible contents, enabled us to attract all the world's major buyers to these shores. If you care to turn around and look out to sea, ladies and gentlemen, or at least visitors to Jum Jum, you will notice that we are being closely observed by some extremely big spenders.'

James was reluctant to obey any instruction issuing from these cursed amplifiers, but he turned towards the shimmering blue waters of the Arafura Sea and sure enough they were dappled with luxury cruisers. He would not have been surprised to learn that Steve Burbek, Agent Stephanie, I. Smirnov, and Colonel Nepfar Alim of the Egyptian Security Services were among the privileged passengers.

'But now, Mr Ball, I will tell you something you do not know and indeed surprisingly have failed even to suspect.' The amplified voice dragged him back to face the infernal arena. 'What you call the theft of the Ashes was affected by a nimble young athlete, skilled in judo and karate, you have come to know and, I understand, to admire as Isha. The Urn she exchanged for a suitable reward with her employer, Ernest Tyburn. The contents she delivered to me. In both cases she betrayed you, as surely as that raddled old whore, Mrs Jan Ball!'

No Japanese rifle butt was raised, but James sank to his knees all the same and settled on the dust where Wally Ficket was still rubbing his shoulder and asking what kind of fancy dress occasion they called this.

'But enough talking, now for the Test Match or if you like the Trial Match,' the amplifiers reverberated on in what seemed now a distant, nightmare world. 'I and my comrades of the Yellow Wombat Brigade will be leaving you very shortly. But that need not stop your fielding practice. In fact, your exertions are just commencing. As you can see, Corporal Lindsay Harrison is loading the bowling machine with fresh balls. One of them is our friend the highly combustible Bouncer. Oh yes, Sir Horace Stoddart flattered himself, indeed he promised Churchill, that he could destroy a city with a missile the size of a cricket ball!

'When he has completed this task, Corporal Harrison will switch the bowling machine to automatic and your practice will commence in earnest. Which ball is the Bouncer? I will have to leave you to judge that for yourselves, but I can promise you it will be worth trying to field it cleanly. The device is triggered by an impact weight of 5 stone 2 pounds, which is the normal pressure of a dropped slip catch. In other words, friends, or at least visitors to Jum Jum, we are giving you a chance, a slim chance; but more than that pom bastard Jardine ever gave me back at MCG!' the voice howled in a spasm of overt Australian. 'A final word. It will be useless to try and join us in our boat or even to swim. Sergeant Kami Tak and his squad will be staying on to supervise your efforts. Their English isn't too good, and in any case they will consider it an honour, after so many years of waiting, to have this oportunity to die for their Emperor.'

'Oh God, they've got a Jap with a machine-gun on the pavilion!' Miles Pershore involuntarily reinforced the grim amplified message.

The Yellow Wombat veterans shouldered arms and, with furtive sidelong glances, moved towards the island's only jetty. There, if James had been looking, he would have seen them form a protective cordon around a grey-haired man of distinctive appearance and retreat with bristling Lee Enfields towards the waiting power cruiser. James was not looking, but he could hear Sandy Winchester's craven cries, and could picture the rest.

'Don't leave without me, I beg you!' the diplomat pleaded, half crawling, half stumbling across the jetty's rickety boards. 'I had absolutely no hand in the regrettable Bodyline series. It was before my time and anyway I would never have condoned those disgraceful tactics. Oh please, listen to me! Between ourselves I'm a little dubious about the stand we took in the War! My wife agrees with me, we should have aimed for a negotiated settlement, particularly with that nice Emperor of Japan. Oh please, gentlemen think of my wife and my two grandsons at Oxford! Listen, I helped you win the First Test at Brisbane. It's true I gave a party for the England team on the eve of the game and did my best to make those bloody poms drunk as skunks – bastards! You see I'm really one of you, you can't leave me behind!'

James only heard the dull thud from a Lee Enfield butt as Sandy Winchester was clubbed into the shallow water at the beach end of the jetty.

James was not looking because for him the world had become a numb void. It was a place without sun, without land, sea or horizons. Whatever was to follow, he knew that in a sense, in all his senses in fact, he was already dead. Without pressing any trigger Marshall had done an effective job of demolition. Only one instinct remained, and it was this that dragged him to his feet and further enabled him to hold out a helping hand to the recumbent Ficket – the place of any man who had ever played first-class cricket had to be with England in their coming ordeal.

Caught and Bowled

The first ball came at them low and fast. Rhodes took it cleanly with a diving catch. Some of the Englishmen crowded round to congratulate him and inspect the projectile, a normal cricket ball as it turned out. This was a mistake because the next ball raced high into a vacated corner of the field. Botham had to gallop yards in reverse to bring off the catch. Then he lost his footing and everyone on the ground held their breath until he surfaced with the missile safely held aloft. This ball, too, had the reassuring name of Slazenger gold-blocked on its circumference.

Wally Ficket was a full cricket pitch away from him, but the next ball or bomb smashed into his stomach.

'For Lord's sake, you kept wicket for England, didn't you?' somebody yelled or implored as the ex-Derby man juggled around his knees with the spinning object.

'Can't take 'em without gloves!' Ficket panted as he subsided with his full weight on top of the dropped catch. Around him every fielder flattened himself. Mercifully the ball was a product of Indian manufacture.

But meanwhile James, and no doubt other shrewd observers on the field, had noted a further inhuman refinement to the automated bowling machine, unadvertised by Marshall – the thing had a rotating muzzle, direction as well as velocity was therefore impossible to predict. Witness Phil Edmonds plucking a scorcher out of the air two hundred yards to Ficket's left. A genuine Gunn and Moore this time.

Now a steepler. Athey, Emburey and Thomas raced to get under it and find themselves on a collision course. Gatting scoops the ball out of their desperate scrum. A Vee-Kay County Special, but it could just as well have been curtains!

'Watch the ball from the moment it leaves the bowler's hand,' they had drummed into James at Wellington and later at Cambridge. And this advice had never seemed more appropriate than now, because the veteran intelligence man was convinced that the Bouncer would not be perfectly round; at some point on its circumference the trigger mechanism would have to show. The only trouble was the 'bowler' was not a hand but a swivelling muzzle and James's eyesight was not what it was.

And yet there was something noticeably different about this cricket ball, whistling like an artillery shell from a German 88. And that's the difference surely: a cricket ball doesn't whistle! Nor for that matter does it dip and swerve so in flight, because a cricket ball is sufficiently round in surface to ensure a reasonably straight trajectory. This ball is behaving erratically because it is weighted on one side by a mechanism. Yes you can see it now – a distinctive metal spur. But, save us, it's cleared your outstretched hand. *The Bouncer!*

Gower manages to get an instep to it and kick it up for Allan Lamb. But the Northants man has thrust himself forward to pick it off David's boot, and now he's too far committed to get back to take a lofted catch. All the same he manages to slow it with his

231

fingers. It ricochets from Lamb in a direction which James has not anticipated. Only a dive can get a hand between the ball and hard earth now. There seems plenty of time because things are now moving in the slow motion of crisis. But by the same token the body is responding with painful slowness. The thing seems to be hanging suspended there, yet the grasping hand is approaching it like a snail.

'Leave it to a professional, James, you bloody ass!' a voice like that of Sir Hector Bootle played at the wrong speed crawls across his consciousness, and the hand which had started ever so slowly to gather the device into its palms is gradually emptying until it has only a fingertip hold, and then none at all. The Bouncer has dropped to earth!'

There was a click, as well as a plop. The certain sound of a mechanism activated, clearly audible in spite of the machine-gun fire. The thing sparked, smoked; then spluttered and became silent and inert. The Bouncer had impacted with the earth; but it was a dead ball.

'Ultimately I believe we owe our salvation to Spooner's relationship with Leopold Jardine,' James explained to the Colonel of Australia's Special Forces in a neat white office in Darwin. 'It was the name, of course, which stuck in his throat. And you might say he killed the goose that could have laid the golden egg. Oh, there can be no doubt but that he killed Leopold Jardine. That cock and bull story about a flying bomb really won't wash, Swindon was miles out of the VI target areas. The trouble was that friend Spooner/Marshall let his anti-English phobia run away with him, as he did this morning. If he had kept his head and waited till Jardine had got his equations right there might have been a point in killing him. As it was, he couldn't wait to vent his spite and, as a result, he got himself an incomplete formula. A bad bargain, but a fortunate result for us.'

'It's a pity we didn't put our heads together earlier about this one, Mr Ball,' said Colonel Loxton of the Australian Special Forces. (His face was still blackened from the successful rescue operation he and his elite troups had mounted at Jum Jum that morning.) 'We've got files this thick on Mr Marsh of the many aliases. We might have been able to help you in the enquiries.'

'Exactly my point, James,' cut in Sir Hector Bootle. 'As always, you thought you knew better than the local security people. You took advice from no one – except from your little friend Isha. A fine friend she turned out to be! It's really quite ironic when you consider all the lectures you've given me on my so-called susceptibility to the fair sex.'

Up until now James's spirits had been stimulated, perhaps artifically, by the excitement of the rescue: the sudden erruption of friendly automatic fire: the swift demolition of Marshall's infernal bowling machine; the Jap machine-gunner tumbling from the blazing pavilion roof – an unsuccessful *hara-kiri* attempt it later transpired; the unceremonious resuscitation of Sandy Winchester (pummelled back into life by his Australian rescuers, he was almost certainly due for a new posting); and finally the exhilarating ride back to Darwin by Hercules transport, shoulder to shoulder with the tired but triumphant England team. But now Hector Bootle had brought him savagely back to earth.

'A discus thrower wasn't she?' Colonel Loxton smiled sternly through his camouflage. 'You wouldn't

233

want to trust her any further than you could throw her, but give her one thing – at least she had the decency to alert us to the situation at Jum Jum. If It's any comfort, Mr Ball, she said she did it for your sake.'

'Knowing, of course, that I was out of harm's way on the golf course with Dennis Lillee and Greg Chappell – at least until you had me radio-paged, Colonel,' Sire Hector elaborated.

James looked up from the khaki carpet. The world was suddenly a fraction warmer. In the open window behind Colonel Loxton he could even glimpse the sun.

'Would it be in order to see her?' he softly enquired.

'Not on Australian territory, I'm afraid, Mr Ball. She was arrested in Brisbane in the early hours of this morning and put on the first plane to Tokyo. Whatever she was up to here, she was doing it without a work permit.'

'Of course, I understand,' James murmured. But in his heart he knew he understood surprisingly little. For instance, he did not understand how almond eyes could look so comprehendingly into the soul, and yet be lying. And given the potential for treason, he could not conceive of a change of heart, certainly not for the sake of a man who was not of her race or creed and was very far from being similar in age. Least of all could he understand how such a delicate, soft hand could find the aggression and brutal power to sunder a Lord's Museum showcase with a single karate chop.

'Naturally you're welcome to see Mr Tyrone Marshall any time you wish,' Colonel Loxton conciliated. 'He'll be behind bars a long time – probably for the rest of his natural life. He and his yellow Wombat mob. Incidentally those old reprobates are going it a bit when they call themselves a "brigade". A platoon was the best they could ever muster, although they tried every POW camp on the River Kwai. I suppose we all have a few rotten apples. You had a Lord called Haw Haw, I'm told.'

'Thank you,' said James, 'but I think I'm already adequately acquainted with Mr Marshall and his Wombat friends.'

'It's the end of quite a trail for us and the police authorities,' Colonel Loxton confessed. 'We've had the Wombat freaks under surveillance since they completed their time in the early '50s. We didn't pull them in again because we knew sooner or later they would lead us to Marsh, who is wanted here on a whole stack of charges – murder and fraud. Between ourselves, we had scheduled a paradrop on Sir Gervase Spooner's Coburn Peninsula hideaway this October – yes, we'd worked that identity change out. What threw us was that obituary notice in *The Times*, which, of course, all our papers copied. We didn't reckon that Marsh was such a skilful chameleon. He'd been running the twin identities of Spooner and his rich neighbour, Tyrone Marshall, for years. So when the Spooner persona became a liability he simply terminated it and put his whole self into Marshall. So you see we'd have found we had quite a lot in common if you'd called on us before.'

'If there's one good thing to have come out of all this,' declared Sir Hector Bootle from the bar stool of the Darwin tavern to which they had adjourned, 'it's that it's become quite clear that you must never be called out of retirement again. In fact, James, I've decided to depart from my principles for once and offer you a substantial "golden goodbye", or rather make it worth your while to stay at home with your begonias, or whatever it is you grow in that St John's

Wood garden, for good. I've decided to overlook Jan's manifest unsuitability, especially since presumably you will have finally seen sense and will be starting divorce proceedings, and will recommend you for a knighthood in the New Year's Honours. If they gave one to Blunt, I'm sure they can stretch a point for you.'

'I suppose I should feel honoured,' answered James from the consolation of a long gin and tonic.

'You're damned right you should,' vehemently agreed Sir Hector. 'I doubt if the KGB would have been so charitable if you'd been in their employ.'

'And yet the world can breathe again. The Urn has been restored. Cricket, though not in the form we reverenced as schoolboys, will continue. We have a few modest grounds for self-congratulations,' James suggested.

'In your position, at this particular moment, James, I would rather doubt it,' said Bootle, raising his eyes to the tavern's door.

A woman had entered, dressed strikingly enough to turn the bushranger hats stretched along the bar. A mass of sleek, black, natural hair, on an artfully fashioned wig, was swept upwards in steepling coiffure held by a giant mother-of-pearl comb. An open fan half disguised the face and accentuated eyebrows. However, both the elaborate hair-style and the silken kimono suggested that when it was lowered oriental features would be revealed.

'Darling, they told me I would find you here,' the apparition spoke. 'You don't have to say anything. I wouldn't blame you if you never talked to me again.'

'Jan!'

'Oh Bally, he was a monster, a perfect beast. I think I must have had a temporary bout of insanity

236

– I mean to imagine I could see anything in him. You know I've never been a snob; but he wasn't even one of Nature's gentlemen. He was a cad, a bully and he didn't play the game.'

'They tell me he could have been better than Bradman,' James answered grimly.

'Bradman would never have left a girl waiting with her bags packed in the foyer of a nighmare hotel in Brisbane, and never even sent a message. I'm sorry, darling, but you'd better hear it from me rather than them, because they're sure to tell you. You see they came to arrest me at dawn; it was all rather degrading and shame-making. They say you may be able to use your influence to get the charges dropped – I'm afraid they include conspiracy and loitering – but at the moment I'm officially on parole.'

'Perhaps you would care to explain the reason for all this,' James gestured towards the wig, the fan and the kimono.

She moved closer to him on uncertain high heels. 'I thought . . . well you see, my darling, I couldn't help hearing about the way your little Esther let you down. Perhaps it was stupid and presumptuous but it occurred to me I might just be able to cushion the shock a little. I know that little girls in kimonos turn you on in a way that I don't – and Bally, my darling, I would so love to turn you on, because I swear to you, my sweetest, you're the only man in the world I really love.'

'Take it off!' James barked. 'Or rather return to your hotel wherever it is and come back in something more suitable to your age and station. And please be quick about it. We are returning to England, tonight if possible!'

'But Bally, the tour has really only just begun. I

hoped that once we got to Perth and put all this behind us, we might . . . well – rediscover each other.'

'Watching cricket out of season has not, when all is said and done, turned out to be a very rewarding experiment,' James reflected. 'We do better to abide by our own seasons.'

'Exactly what I've always told you, James,' nodded Sir Hector Bootle.

'In fact,' James told his wife masterfully, 'you'd better dress in something warm. If we can catch a plane out of Australia this evening we could just be in time to see the first England trial at Twickenham.'

Postscripts

A few minutes before James Ball boarded his QUANTAS flight he was handed a letter with a scarlet MCC stamp. It read as follows:

Dear Ball,

I understand from Sir Hector Bootle's cable that you were of some assistance to him in his spectacular retrieval of the priceless Ashes Urn. You will readily imagine the unalloyed joy this intrepid feat has caused here at Head-quarters, not least to me personally and to my Museum staff who, if our principal admissions-earner had not been replaced, would have been faced with serious but necessary redundancies.

The popular press possibly exaggerates the significance to the nation of the recovery of the Ashes at a difficult time for the economy and the game, but there can be no doubt that your contribution merits a hearty note of appreciation.

I would consider it an honour when you return to England if you would care to have lunch with me. They do an excellent moussaka at the Tavern public house by the Grace Gate and of course it is extremely convenient for me, being just a short stroll from my office above the Club's treasures.

Again my very cordial thanks.

Sir Wilfred Breslau,
Senior Antiquarian, MCC.

A few weeks later, publishing executives of Collins (Willow), Kingswood (Heinemann), Stanley Paul and

Pavilion Books were scanning with bitterness and some self-recrimination the following whole-page advertisement in *The Bookseller*, 'The Organ of The Book Trade':

Exclusively from Weidenfeld and Nicolson – the sensational true story of Bodyline's first casualty:

FIRST KNOCK
By Sebastian Gover

There have been other cricket books. But never one to match the excitement, drama and breathtaking impact of *First Knock*. It reads like fiction at its most compelling; but it happens to be true. Here is the scarcely believable but fully authenticated story of Ron Marsh, batsman and Bodyline victim turned international espionage agent and leading world criminal.

It is a unique rags to illegal riches saga, laced with violence, treason, passion and betrayal, which propels the reader from humble beginnings in Sunbury, Victoria, through war-torn Singapore to top-secret research in Churchill's Britain, and on to a knighthood-winning assignment with Royalty and undreamed of wealth in off-shore oil speculation. *Only* Sebastian Gover is qualified to tell Ron Marsh's astonishing story, because *only* Sebastian Gover has obtained unique access to Marsh in his Australian prison cell.

First Knock contains his exclusive revelations as told to superlative cricket writer and investigative journalist Sebastian Gover!

★ Major author tours with media interviews

★ Multi-media subsidiary rights already negotiated

★ SOON TO BE A MAJOR MOTION PICTURE